A CRASH COURSE IN STARTING A BUSINESS

CRASH COURSE for ENTREPRENEURS

A CRASH COURSE IN STARTING A BUSINESS

Learn What You Need in Two Hours

Scott L. Girard, Jr., Michael F. O'Keefe
and Marc A. Price

A Crash Course for Entrepreneurs

Series Editor: Scott L. Girard, Jr.

A Crash Course for Entrepreneurs—From Expert Business Advice

Starting a Business

Sales and Marketing

Managing Your Business

Business Finance

Legal Aspects of Entrepreneurship

Franchising

Value-Driven Business

Time and Efficiency

International Business

Supplemental Income

Social Media

Web-Based Business

For Gaye, Lynda, Marci and Stef

Contents

Foreword   13

Chapter I: Planning   17
    Entrepreneur: Do You Have What It Takes?   19
    What Business Is Best for You?   21
    Five Boxes to Check *Before* Starting a Business   23
    I've Got a Great Idea! What Next?   25
    Choosing the Best Type of Business   27
    Do I Need a Business License for My Home Business?   29
    How to Create a New Business or Product Name   31
    The Difference Between Partners and Investors   33
    An Overview of How to Write a Business Plan   35
    A Detailed View of How to Write a Business Plan   39
    A.T.N.A. (All Talk, No Action)   53
    Prioritizing Your Way to Success   55
    The Importance of Market Testing   57
    The Four Worst Entrepreneurial Mistakes   59

Chapter II: Getting Financed   61
    How to Obtain Business Financing   63
    The Transformation of Lending   67
    Building a Financial Foundation for Your Business   69
    Getting Your Business the Credit it Deserves   73

Chapter III: Getting Started   77
    Stage of Business Balanced with Speed of Business   79
    How to Blue Chip Your Business   83
    Designing a Logo to Establish Your Brand and Image   85
    The Importance of Domain Names   87
    The Difference Between Copyrights and Trademarks   89
    How to Patent a New Product   91
    "The Name's Bond—Surety Bond"   95
    The Greatest Start-Up Challenges   97

Chapter IV: Stayin' Alive   99
         Getting Business in Old and New Ways   101
         The Importance of Legal and Accounting Representation   103
         How to Write a Press Release   105
         Small Business Tax Tips   107
         Hiring: Talent, Loyalty and Age   109

Chapter V: When Tomorrow Becomes Today   111
         Starting a Web-Based Business   113
         Making Sure People Find Your Internet Business   115

Afterword: Where to Go from Here?   119

Acknowledgements   121

Glossary   123

Resources   146

Index   149

About the Authors   155

Foreword

You can spot entrepreneurs easily when they talk about their businesses and dreams. Their passion and fascination with their business – and others' businesses – is remarkable. When I met Scott, Mike and Marc, I knew before they told me about the 17 businesses they've collectively started that these were talented, insightful, seasoned entrepreneurs. We quickly agreed to develop the Crash Course for Entrepreneurs together.

The aim of this series is to give you high-level overviews of the critical things you need to know and do if you want to start (or you're already running) your own business. In a two-hour read. Of course, there's much more to know about every topic covered, but we believe that what you'll read here will give you the framework for learning the rest. A Resources section and a Glossary will ensure you can ground yourself in the essentials. And www.expertbusinessadvice.com, the co-authors' website, offers expanded support for entrepreneurs that is updated daily.

Entrepreneurs vary widely in what they want to do. Your dream may be to start a very small, one-person service, perhaps doing home maintenance or day care or accounting from your home. You may have developed or discovered a high-tech breakthrough that will need years of testing and dozens or hundreds of people to bring to market. This book sees the intrinsic value and challenges of both styles of business. It will definitely help you make the most of your opportunity, whatever its scale.

Most of the chapters in this book represent the authors' collective experience and point of view, but a few are personal pieces. You'll find the initials of each author at the end of those. Here's a brief word from each of them.

I remember when I fully understood what our series of books should accomplish. Mike, Marc and I had only decided that we wanted to write a series of books for people only moderately familiar with entrepreneurship and business. Multitudes of books already exist on basic levels of business practices and procedures. We knew that writing another one of those books wouldn't really serve anyone or change anything, no matter how well written it was.

On the morning that I "got it," I was drinking coffee and reading the news; the television was on in the background. I glanced up and saw a commercial for a foreign language software program in which, instead of learning by simply repeating vocabulary, the student is culturally immersed in the language, holistically surrounded with concepts of all manner of things applicable to the subject. In short, they don't list facts and terms and call it teaching—they show the student a vast array of information, on a multitude of levels, allowing her to bathe in knowledge.

I knew then that instead of presenting a bunch of facts that we think you should know about business, we should take a more holistic approach and help you immerse yourself in business thinking. Our method is most effective if you read this book cover to cover, skipping nothing. If you reach a section and either think it doesn't address your needs, or you think you know everything there is to know about the subject, read it anyway. It'll only take a minute—that's why the sections are not lengthy. It will enlighten and organize your thinking, either way. You'll see important concepts woven through various discussions, as they holistically fit in.

If you're hoping to read a book and immediately become the world's greatest business person, this book isn't for you. If your goal, however, is to quickly understand and feel familiar with the basics of starting a business, as your first stepping-stone to greatness, we believe that our book has no rival.

I sincerely hope that this book will not only increase your understanding of entrepreneurship and starting a business, but that it also gives you pleasure and satisfaction as you learn the key principles and language of business.

Scott L. Girard, Jr.

When we sat down and decided to take on the daunting task of writing a series of books for entrepreneurs and small business owners, I cringed. I thought, "How can we ever reduce our advice and experiences to writing? And how can we cover it all—can we fit it into a book?"

Either way, we decided to get started, so each of us began drafting sections related to our respective specialties and work experience. Only as the initiative continued did I discover a certain passion for sharing my advice in a personal way, trying to convey how it felt to go places, negotiate situations, and experience new things, both good and bad, in the course of starting businesses.

I hope that this book will capture your interest, provide valuable information, and share an interesting perspective into the world of entrepreneurship and small business conception.

Mike F. O'Keefe

Everyone has heard the phrase "Knowledge is Power." I would have it read "Information is Power," for a couple of reasons.

We live in an age of instant information about every facet of our lives. We can receive news, on-demand weather and traffic reports, sports scores, social media happenings, and stock market updates. And yet, we forget much of this information within moments of receiving it, as new reports and updates are constantly replacing the data we were just beginning to process.

Most generic information travels fast these days. On the other hand, some information is meant to stay with us for a while, if not forever. And with that in mind, Scott, Mike and I set out to write a series of books to deliver lasting, valid information for entrepreneurs and small business people.

Our passion for success in business and in life lies behind every page we write. As life-long, serial entrepreneurs, we have always taken the approach of surrounding ourselves with information, ideas and viewpoints from countless sources to support our efforts in constructing our next project. That information, when reliable and trustworthy, can and will be used over and over for repeated success. So, in essence, information is power, when applied over time.

Our series of books represents the hard work, research and application of numerous business philosophies, ideas and viewpoints. You will find rock-solid information that can be applied now…and later. It's information that can be shared, and then referred to as a refresher down the road, if needed. Our goal was to deliver information and advice that is relevant, smart and timely. We hope these fresh, contemporary approaches to the fundamentals of business will get you, and keep you, at the top of your game.

The way forward begins here…

Marc A. Price

We all hope this book supports the fire and drive you feel now as you think about starting or confront the realities of running your own business day to day. And we wish you success.

Kathe Grooms
Managing Director, Nova Vista Publishing

CHAPTER I
Planning

Entrepreneur: Do You Have What It Takes?

In an economy when so many fail, do you have what it takes to succeed?

I LIKE TO THINK that somewhere deep inside almost everyone, there is a potential entrepreneur. For entrepreneurs, survival becomes a very real challenge. Yet humans have survived millions of years, when so many other species haven't. We are an intelligent and adaptable group of fighters and survivors. While I believe that most people can be successful entrepreneurs if they truly want to, it's the *want* that stops them. They confuse it with *can't*. The truth is that you really *can*, but not without sacrifices and the right resources. At the end of the day, most people aren't willing to dig in and fight the long, hard battle to realize success.

Some say that starting a business in today's economy is harder than it's ever been. Some say otherwise. The facts are clear: Financial resources are plentiful to help a hopeful entrepreneur become successful. The market, however, is so saturated that getting a piece of those resources only comes to those who are willing to fight for it.

The first step is looking inside yourself and deciding if you are the type of person who shows the most common traits of successful entrepreneurs.

1. Are you motivated to get things done? Do you act before someone has to tell you to get going? These are very important traits for an entrepreneur, because you're the one at the helm. Not only do you have to be comfortable motivating yourself, but also motivating others. You're the boss now, so get used to it.

2. Are you easily intimidated? Do you tend to avoid competition? If so, you may want to reconsider starting a business. Intimidation and com-

petition will fly at you from all directions and in all different forms. Other businesses, time, paperwork, changing conditions, money— they are all adversaries in your new endeavor and have real potential to make you fail.

3.   Are you a good, open-minded listener? Part of being a good leader is being a good listener. We weren't born knowing everything, so part of being a successful entrepreneur is being able to listen and take advice from others. Quite frankly, you'd be foolish not to.

4.   Do you know yourself well? Take an honest look at yourself. Having a solid understanding of your own strengths and weaknesses is probably the most important part of your pre-launch self-evaluation. When things get tough (and believe me, they will, at some point), you must have the will-power and self-discipline to overcome challenges, as well as the ability to assess risk and make decisions quickly in order to mitigate that risk.

5.   Do you know what you're getting into? This question opens out into lots of related questions: Do you have the energy to push your business ahead ? Are your personal assets mostly positive (like your emotional or other support from family and friends, knowledge of the area of your proposed business, a business environment that at least is not hostile to your dream)? Is the type of business you picture realistic, given your abilities and the resources you can imagine tapping?

The bottom line here is that not everyone will start and run a business. Not exactly because they *can't*, per se, but because they *won't*. Some people just aren't willing to give it their all. The scariest part of it is that people who tell themselves that they will not give up, no matter what, sometimes end up giving up anyway because the struggles they face down the line are greater than they ever imagined.

Starting and running your own business can be a dream come true. At last, you can be yourself and run your own show. You don't have to share the wealth (unless you want to) and you can make all of your own decisions.

Keep these final thoughts in mind: starting a business is harder than you think it will be, but it's not impossible. Your mistakes are not failures—they're lessons. Learn from them and move on. People all over the world start successful businesses every single day. Are they better than you? Absolutely not! You have what it takes somewhere inside you to be successful; right now. So if you're ready for the challenge, reach down deep and don't let go until you've arrived where you want to be.

What Business is Best for You?

*Every entrepreneur's first question is seldom the easiest.
Here are some tips to help you decide and get you
pointed in the right direction.*

HERE'S A TRUE STORY. For the first three years of college, I was an international business and economics double-major. I was setting myself up to be a major player in the global business scene. My grades were stellar and it was looking like I'd land a great job right out of school. I had done extremely well in my summer internships and had proven myself to many leaders in the business circles I had ventured into.

There was one problem. Over the years, I had grown to loathe working in international business. Although I was still excelling, it was a matter of principle, not passion. In short, I grew to learn that international business was *not* the best choice for me to pursue, especially if I wanted to go into business for myself.

Making a career choice certainly requires honesty. Do you really want to be an investment banker? Lawyer? Doctor? Or do you actually want to be an art director, product designer, daycare owner, racecar driver, whatever? Look inside yourself and decide what you would really *love* to do for a living. I'm not going to lie to you and say that that's all you have to do—I don't buy that "If you can dream it, you can do it" boloney. But seriously, deciding what you truly want to do is the first step in starting the right business for you.

If, like so many others, you really don't know what you love to do (it may sound silly, but it's an extremely common problem for would-be entrepreneurs), think back about what you're good at. People usually like to do what they're good at. What did you achieve awards for as you were growing up? What were your hobbies? On what do you receive compliments from others?

Suppose someone on the street stopped you and said, "Listen, I've got more money than I know what to do with and I want to bankroll whatever business you want. I'll pay you more than you've ever dreamed to do it". What would you answer? What kind of business would you choose to start?

So let's say you can name a few dreams. As we all know, it's not quite as simple as dreaming and doing. The next step, of course, is to conduct research or rational brainstorming to test whether your dream is plausible or even possible. For instance, if you're fifty years old, I'm sorry—you're not going to be a professional basketball star. If you want to open a surf shop but live in the middle of the desert, I don't believe you'll be selling many surfboards there. Market testing is a very important aspect of deciding what kind of business is best for you.

So what happened in my story? I changed my major at the beginning of my senior year and, although I still earned minor degrees in international business and economics, my new major was in my true passion: writing. Although it was scary at first, I now know that I made the right choice, despite the risks. Why? Because I'm making a very good living doing what I love to do. I will always have my knowledge and insight into the global business and economic arenas, but I now use my passion and talents in my own business to write about what I know and to convey my knowledge to others, on my terms, and in my own voice. My father always said that if you love what you do, you'll never work a day in your life.

You know what? He was right.

S.G.

Five Boxes to Check
Before Starting a Business

You're not just a soon-to-be entrepreneur; you're also a person with a life. Don't screw it up by jumping the gun on your new business.

PEOPLE GET SO EXCITED when they feel like they've connected all of the intellectual dots and now have a complete idea about how to get their new business off the ground. Maybe they finally figured out the chemical composition of their new product, or finally just thought of the perfect name for their business.

Whatever the last piece of the puzzle was, don't let it excite you to the point where you get tunnel vision and lose sight of short-term goals. Before you go quitting your day job to start your new business, you need to ensure that you can check these five boxes so that you don't end up right back at your old desk.

- ☐ Do you have enough money to live on while you start up? It might sound silly, but sometimes people get so wrapped up thinking about money for their new business that they forget to think about other important expenses that they will still be expected to pay, like rent, a mortgage, food, car, insurance, etc. Can you cover them while you're getting your business started? Experts say that having six months of living expenses saved up is a safe estimate, but the nature of our new business may require you to have more than that. Just make sure that you're not calling your living expenses start-up capital, or vice-versa.

- ☐ Have you checked out your proposed location? Just because an idea is awesome doesn't mean that it's awesome for the location where you're starting a business. Snowshoe companies don't do well in Kuwait, gardeners for hire don't do well in Antarctica, and a used car parts shop in a rich neighborhood probably won't attract a single customer. The reasons why certain establishments don't survive in certain markets are countless. Sometimes, people find out the hard way by going out of business. Research other businesses like yours in the area in which you want to open, and see how they're doing.

☐   Have you written a business and a marketing plan? Do you have any kind of plan at all? If so, is it good enough? Have you covered all of your bases? While part of writing a plan is organization and clarifying what you expect to do, the other major part is uncovering hidden issues or things you may not have thought of.

☐   Test the water before you dive in. If you have your day job, try working as much as you can toward your new endeavor at night. This ties directly to Point Two above, in that you may be able to conduct a full market test through working at night and on the weekends while you still have your day job. If you can manage this for just a little while, it's a great way to maintain your life's security while testing whether or not your new endeavor will work.

☐   Plan the transition. Brainstorming the strategy that takes you from where you are today to being an entrepreneur in the future will surely cause you to revise and revise your business plan. And that's good. No one, no matter how smart, can effectively plan the transition in one try. There are simply too many facets, including ones that you can't learn from books and that may be specific and unique to your personal life, to keep track of all at once. The biggest by far is your finances.

This can be daunting because not only do you have to consider your new business finances, but also your personal finances. Typically, things don't go as planned. You need to have contingency plans in place for your life's vitals like health, vehicle and home-owners insurance, child care, mortgage, etc.

Of course, not everyone who is trying to start a business is currently employed. However, the same general rules apply. Stabilize yourself before you try to start and stabilize a new business. If you have to work a job that you don't really enjoy for a short time, just to pay your bills and allow yourself to live while you start your own business at night or on the weekends, so be it. If you have enough money saved to start your own business without working a second job, that's even better. Just ensure that you don't run out of money before your new business can support you. Keep in mind that there's a big difference between your business being cash-flow positive and being able to support yourself.

It's important to stay on top of your personal finances during the transition period from employee to entrepreneur. While no one wants to think about it, in case your endeavor doesn't make it, you don't want to have to look for a new job while trying to put your personal life back together, too. But if you can check these five key boxes before you make your moves, you'll have far better odds of succeeding.

I've Got a Great Idea!
What Next?

What to do with great business and product ideas.

IT'S A PROBLEM no one ever expects to have. Everyone who sits around trying to think of a good business or product idea never considers what to do once they have one. When the light bulb flashes, inventors and soon-to-be entrepreneurs get a look of sheer excitement because they're sure that they've finally thought of the idea that will make them a ton of money. Soon, however, they realize that while they do have a great idea, what they don't have is a plan or task list to get their product launched or their business idea to the next level. Often, they don't even know what the next level is. If you've been in this boat, don't be discouraged. Most people are, or have been in it too.

Depending on whether you're basing your new business on a tangible product, a service, or an intellectual property, the second step (after thinking of the idea) is to decide if you need to protect it with a patent, trademark, copyright, or any combination of them. A seasonal cherry pie road stand probably doesn't need protection, but suppose that stand is so successful that you want to take it to the next stage. Your hand-painted logo may need trademark protection if you plan to upsize your operation.

If you live in the US, the United States Patent and Trademark Office (USP-TO) website will give you all the information and services you need to protect your product, service or idea. Similar offices do the same things in other countries. Once your idea is protected, you can get started planning and acquiring financing.

Not everyone with a great idea, however, wants to start a business. Writers don't write books because they want to start a publishing company, after all. Many people, after coming up with a great idea, want to put it on the open market, sell it, come up with another great idea, and repeat the entire process.

It can be tricky selling something on the open market, especially to large corporations. They have entire staffs of people whose jobs it is to write the best contracts or negotiate the best deals on behalf of the company so that, above all else, the company comes out on top in its purchases.

If this is your strategy, after making contact with the corporation, secure a fully executed non-disclosure agreement from them. The point of contact for this should be a duly authorized officer who can bind the company to the terms and conditions of your non-disclosure and acknowledge the presence of your copyright protection. We recommend that you secure this acknowledgement with two steps: the executed non-disclosure agreement, and a signature of acceptance on a letter you draft that requests their acknowledgment of certain specific points (e.g., copyright) that are important to you.

If they accept your terms, they will ask you to sign a contract. Although you may think you understand the terms stated in the contract, you would be wise to have legal representation of your own look it over before you sign it.

Once the legalities are taken care of, the hard part is generally over. No matter how excited you are about it, the safety and security of your great idea should be solidly protected.

That applies to you equally if your strategy is to develop rather than sell your idea. While it remains yours, do watch out for unfair use, piracy, copying, and so forth. Even with the protection of patent, trademark or copyright law, it does not mean your rights could be innocently or otherwise infringed upon by others. So always be alert to potential threats to your great new idea.

Choosing the Best Type of Business

When conceptualizing a new venture, entrepreneurs must consider which type of business will suit it best. Start your business the right way by addressing this first.

YOU PAY BILLS EVERY month to businesses like Jack's Garage, Tax Prep LLC, and Green Utility Corporation. Each of these businesses has a unique corporate structure. When you set up yours, you need to pick the best type of business structure to suit your great idea.

Whether you set up your business as a sole proprietorship, partnership, limited liability company (LLC), S-Corporation, or C-Corporation, it is vital to understand not only the filing and paperwork requirements, but also the different tax implications and liability impacts that each type of business structure entails.

Sole proprietorships: Commonly, owner-operated small businesses are set up as sole proprietorships due to the simplicity of the filings and regulation, as well as the single-layer tax impact on the revenues of the business. This type of ownership also allows you, the owner, to be your own boss. However, you should be extremely cautious if you set up either as a sole proprietor or in a general partnership. Both types of business structures allow for all of the liabilities of the business to be shared with the individual owners on a personal level. Unlimited liability can be scary. Just remember to hope for the best but plan for the worst. Don't choose a business structure based on the ease and convenience of setting it up.

It is more common than one would think to have business situations end in lawsuits resulting in general partners and sole proprietors being sued personally and losing homes, cars and savings accounts. There are plenty of hurdles that these types of business owners have to overcome. Management can be difficult with limited participants and there is commonly an overwhelming time commitment associated with this type of business.

* While the examples and names of types of businesses in this section are from the United States, the general structure of businesses is much the same worldwide.

Partnerships: There are two types of members in a partnership—a general partner and a limited partner. General partners have unlimited liability and are typically managers of the company. Limited partners have exactly what you would think—limited liability, and they usually do not have a role managing the company. Just remember, no matter how well the individual partners get along, one of the most common issues with partnerships is the disagreements that arise between members. This sometimes leads to unfortunate fallings-out among friends.

Corporations: Most successful types of businesses are corporations—either limited liability companies (LLCs), conventional corporations (C-Corporations), or S-Corporations. These three forms of business ownership generate approximately 80 percent of all sales in the United States and they all share two major benefits. First, they have limited liability, and second, they usually qualify for special tax advantages that other types of business ownerships do not enjoy.

Incorporating a business is a great strategy. It allows for the company to grow, it has perpetual life, makes change of ownership easy, and it's common for corporations to be able to afford talented employees. However, there are some disadvantages to incorporating a business. Corporations cost more to start than sole proprietorships or partnerships, they require more paperwork, and conflicts among owners and board members can arise. They are also affected by double taxation, which means that the business's profits will be taxed, as well as the shareholders' dividends.

A limited liability company (LLC) is a form of business in which owners and managers receive the limited liability and tax benefits of an S Corporation without having to conform to the S corporation restrictions. For certain professions, e.g., accounting, architecture, and medical or psychological care, the LLC becomes a PLLC, a professional limited liability company.

A special type of incorporation is called an S-Corporation. Aside from sharing the benefit of limited liability, this type of corporation has a major difference from a conventional C-Corporation. It has much simpler taxes, called *single taxation*, that are similar to those of a partnership. Downsides of incorporating as an S-Corporation include ineligibility for a dividends-received deduction, and that S-Corps are not subject to the 10 percent of taxable income limitation that are applicable to charitable contribution deductions.

Choosing the best type of business is a personal choice, and it's certainly one that shouldn't be taken lightly. This is an area where professional advice, tailored to your locality and business sector, is essential. Seriously analyze your business's projected longevity, growth and future development before making your choice.

Do I Need a Business License for My Home Business?

*Tips for getting the paperwork aspect out of the way
so you get on to making money at home!*

DEPENDING ON THE TYPE of business you are starting, you may be required to obtain local, county, state (or provincial) or national licensing. Since heavy fines are usually associated with conducting a business without proper licenses and permits, it is important to determine which licenses will be required before you start conducting business.

Naturally, different localities can have different business licensing requirements. A good source of information is the Internet, specifically your local, county, state, or federal government websites. Not only will they provide answers to all the questions you might have, but they will have contact information and downloadable documents and even tutorials so that you can begin the process immediately at home. In many cases, you will only have to show up at an office and sign the document. It's even possible, in some cases, that you can complete the entire process at home via the Internet or by postal applications.

In general, most small and home-based businesses will only require a local business license or permit. It's important to conduct research and get authoritative answers, however, because the last thing you want is to be held up by red tape or fees when you're trying to launch a new business.

Certain business categories, like for example, a restaurant that offers liquor, may require multiple licenses and even inspections. These licenses can be very expensive and the penalties and fees for serving alcohol without a license can cost more than the license itself. Some localities even have jail time rolled up with the punishment. In short, don't serve alcohol without a license; it's not worth it. Enough said.

If you intend to start a home-based business, ensure that, aside from acquiring a business license, you check local zoning requirements (this can typically also be accomplished at your local courthouse or town hall) as well as any property covenants or rental contracts that apply. Zoning requirements regulate how property can be used, and some activities may not be allowed in your area. A typical problem for a home-based startup is that the owner's apartment rental contract prohibits conducting business from the place. Here again, don't risk punishments and penalties that will hold up your launch and mar your credibility as a business person.

Some types of businesses may require a state or provincial license. Examples include attorneys, barbers, contractors, dentists and social workers. Each state has an agency dealing with these types of businesses. You can determine if your business requires such a license by contacting your local government offices.

For a very few businesses, a national license is required, e.g. for those engaged in providing investment advice or dealing with firearms. In general, a national licensing is required if the business is highly regulated by the government. It is best to consult an attorney in these cases.

Naturally, as an entrepreneur, you're eager to get going on the business itself. But tell yourself to be patient and get these formalities out of the way early in your start-up process. Once they are done, you'll soon forget the time and effort they require.

How to Create a New Business or Product Name

If you think naming children is hard, just try naming your business or product. It should be smart and functional.

WHILE NAMES MAY SEEM like a tiny detail, they are actually very important. "Just give it a name and sell it," some people say. And while their assertiveness is admirable, the name of your new business or product deserves a bit more thought than that. Sometimes, your first instinct is the best one, and other times, it can take days, weeks, or longer to really settle on the perfect name.

The general intent of a business or product name is to describe the product or company while being memorable and desirable to the person who reads or sees it. There are just as many ways to come up with a good name as there are reasons why you need one. For marketing, it's vital. A good name will draw people to your product or company and thus, the product will be more likely to sell itself. That way, your company may have to spend less on publicity.

We all know when we see a good business or product name. Several patterns have evolved over time. While some people see alliteration (two or more words that start with the same sounding letter) as kitsch, others see it as clever, e.g., Coca-Cola, Kandy Kitchen, Best Buy, Dunkin' Donuts, etc. Same goes for business or product names that consist of two or more words that rhyme.

So, where do I start?

Think about your new business or product and decide what message you want to send through it. If you are starting your own law practice, then Jennie's One-Stop Law Shop just won't be credible. If you want to open a boxing gym, would you even consider naming it, "Sissy Mary's Boxing Gym"? Of course not. You would want something tough-sounding, like "Lights Out Boxing Center".

What do you know about your industry and the people who patronize it? If you're trying to start something new, chances are you probably already know quite a bit about what works and what doesn't. Think about what conventions apply to names in your kind of business. Use that knowledge and be creative while still sounding credible.

Sometimes, less is more. There is a barbershop in my area called "Tim's Gentlemen's Haircuts," and the place is wildly popular. Tim is the owner and he cuts hair. Enough said. Depending on your product or business, this could work well for you. Sometimes, certain clientele respond better to the direct approach and the sense of personal involvement of the owner, shown through the use of his name.

What is the nature or origin of your product or service? Sometimes, researching these things can open up a lot of wonderful name ideas. Did the concept begin in another country? While writing a business plan for a friend of mine a few years ago for an imported wine, cheese and meat shop plus café that he wanted to open, I suggested that he consider "La Bonne Vie," French for "The Good Life," for the name of the shop. It worked on multiple levels because his products fit the French feel; the name's concept fits the area—a quiet, but upscale, part of town—and it suggested how consuming his products makes you feel. So naming the shop La Bonne Vie fit perfectly.

Sometimes people ask me what the best business name I've ever seen is. While there are many brilliant business names out there, my very favorite is a tiny, independently-owned mechanic shop near my house named "Honest Engine Mechanic Shop". Their logo is a smiling cartoon Native American holding a wrench in one hand and waving with the other. Brilliant.

The bottom line here is that while thinking of a name for a new product or business is very important, it should also be something you can have fun doing. Don't rush it, but if after a while if you still can't think of anything, there are business and product naming software options and consultants that can assist you.

One final thought: ensure that before you have settled on a name for your new business, you do a thorough online search to ensure that a company or product hasn't already claimed and protected that name with copyright or trademark law. It can save you tons of money in legal fees and the re-creation of marketing plans and materials down the road.

S.G.

The Difference Between Partners and Investors

This choice is one of the most important ones you will make. A lot depends on how much and what kind of involvement you want others to have in your company.

WHEN YOU ARE looking for financing for your business, understanding the difference between partners and investors is very important. Both can help you raise the necessary funds that you need to start and operate your business. However, they play very different roles in the business.

An *investor* will basically put money into a business in hopes of getting some returns on his investment. On the other hand, business *partners* co-own a business. They raise the capital for the business per agreed terms. This is probably the biggest difference between partners and investors. Business partners share losses and profits while investors expect returns on their investment regardless of how well the business is doing. The business owner will shoulder the losses and ensure that the investors get good returns on their investment.

Another major difference between partners and investors regards running the business. Normally, investors will not participate in the day-to-day running of the business. However, you need to keep them informed of everything: in particular, the accounts of the company. They want to know how you are spending their money, how the business is performing, and the returns accrued or expected. On the other hand, your business partner has to be involved in all the business operations. You and your partner may play different roles, but you have to both be involved in the decision making.

General partnerships mean that all the business partners share all the business responsibilities equally. For instance, this means that profits and losses are equally shared among all of them. If the business experiences any major problems, all partners must accept liability. That means that if they fail to pay taxes and are arrested, all of them are answerable. Of course, if four partners own a business together, they do not all have to own an equal share. One partner can own 50 percent, while the others split the remaining 50 percent among them. However, from a responsibility standpoint, when it comes to the investors, they have no obligations to share any responsibilities with the business owners. The difference between partners and investors is that the former is responsible for the business while the latter is not.

A word on percentages of ownership is in order here. If you want to control your business, make sure you own 51 percent or more of its shares. Your partners therefore can never outvote you on serious decisions.

The liability of the partners may be limited when it comes to limited partnerships (LLC's). However, there is still at least one partner who has to accept unlimited liability for the company.

In some cases, investors may also be partners. For instance, an angel investor (see page 66) may ask for a share of the company instead of asking for returns on his investment. This is normally based on how he perceives the business's potential and also his own interest in the business. The difference between partners and investors is that while one party assumes immediate co-ownership of the business, the other can decide not to co-own the business at all.

Understanding the difference between partners and investors is important, especially when you need to know where you can get your financing. Both can be very helpful to a business, but you need to carry out adequate research in order to decide whether to get financing from partners, investors or, if possible, fund the whole thing yourself.

An Overview of How to Write a Business Plan

*The best way to start this large and important project
is to understand the basic elements.*

AS YOU ALREADY have seen, a sound business plan is critical to your success as an entrepreneur. Preparing it frankly requires a lot of work, but the exercise repays you by reducing the number of things that can surprise you, shining light on aspects of your intentions, plans or resources that are shaky, and developing your confidence that you've done your homework and are ready for the big test.

Of course, your plan will reflect the level of complexity and scope of the business you are starting. But even if you are simply opening a hotdog stand, it pays to think through all the applicable parts and have clearly stated, written answers worked out. That stand may become the next big hot dog chain! And you will find that supplying the expected information will sharpen your own vision and give you a greater sense of ownership in the business you are starting.

So the first and most important reader of your business plan is *you*. You will probably go back to this document again and again as you move forward. Consider it a changeable road map. But your plan also may be read by potential partners, banks, investors, key hires, organizations which grant subsidies, and so forth. Below are the key elements; in the next chapter we'll take each one up in detail.

The EXECUTIVE SUMMARY is a brief paragraph that describes your company and its industry sector. Include any industry standards and statistics that support your reasons for expecting your business's success. If you are adapting your plan for a funding request, at the start of this paragraph, clearly state the total capital requirements requested of the reader (investor, bank, etc.).

The MARKET ANALYSIS portion is a detailed profile of your target market and its consumers. The more *relevant* data you can gather to support your claim that your target market is in need of your new product or business, the better.

In the COMPANY DESCRIPTION portion, provide the reader with an understanding of your company's business structure, e.g., corporation, limited liability company, sole proprietorship. Also include your mission statement, continuing with a sentence or two that details the planned direction of the organization for the next few years. Close this section with the most current mailing address and contact information of the business and key players.

Create an ORGANIZATION AND MANAGEMENT section, introducing the reader to the founders and other noteworthy participants in the business. Provide a detailed description of the persons listed above, explaining their titles, involvement, experience, qualifications and pertinent supplementary information. If your business includes more than one level of participants, an organization chart would be useful.

In the MARKETING AND SALES STRATEGY section, the first thing you want to do is define your marketing strategy. There is no single way to approach a marketing strategy. However, there are common steps you can follow to help you think through the direction and tactics you plan to use to go to market, drive sales and sustain customer loyalty.

An overall marketing strategy should include, at a minimum, four separate strategy statements for your market penetration, growth, distribution, and communication.

Include any pertinent demographic research and industry trends and profiles. Touch on the different market segments you plan to sell to, and how you plan to approach them. Include plans as needed for appropriate local, regional, national, international and web-based marketing. If a website is in the plan, this is where you should outline its development, including consumer imagery, functionality and search engine optimization (SEO). Discuss the media you will use, including back-up plans in case revenues can't fund all the activity you plan. Then separately discuss the different marketing and advertising campaigns you plan within each type of media.

Next, define your sales strategy: how you plan to actually sell your products or services. Include two primary elements: your sales force strategy and your sales activities.

In the SERVICE OR PRODUCT LINE section, introduce the reader to your key products or services. Lay out the idea behind each, and detail what makes it a value to your potential customers. Also, explain why yours are better than products or services offered by the competition. Follow this introduction with individual breakdowns of each product or service, if you plan multiple offerings.

In the FUNDING REQUEST section, if that's what you are using this version for, take this opportunity to educate your reader on the direction your team plans to take the business, how much it will cost to get there, and how you will use the funding you are requesting. Make this section read like an internal document, similar to an employee handbook. Give a synopsis of future sales expectations, expansion of the marketing plan, and employee growth. This is where well thought-out ideas regarding streamlining production, promotion and distribution are presented (consider outsourcing, private labeling, licensing, trade marking, and franchising).

The final section, FINANCIALS, is the most crucial to the success of your new business. Create this document to ensure you have done the appropriate research and financial planning to start and operate your business. Include all fixed and variable expenses, then match these numbers with all expected revenue sources. After producing a narrative summary of these items, you will need to prepare the necessary expense reports, including balance sheets, income statements (or forecasts), statements (or forecasts) of cash flow, and pro forma income statements.

Remember, too, that you should include a private placement disclaimer with your business plan if you plan to use it to raise capital. Private placement is the sale of securities directly to an institutional investor, such as a bank, mutual fund, foundation, insurance company, etc. It does not require Securities Exchange Commission (SEC) registration, provided that the securities are purchased for investment purchases only, not for resale. The private placement disclaimer specifies this fact.

Following the Financials section, you may need to include an APPENDIX. It can contain relevant back-up documents like agreements, reports, résumés, and the like.

All copies of your business plan should be controlled, so ensure that you keep a distribution record. This will allow you to update and maintain your business plan on an as-needed basis.

A Detailed View of How to Write a Business Plan

Writing a business plan is the most important facet of starting a business. Consequently, it's also the greatest deterrent for some entrepreneurs. Fear not.

AFTER YOU HAVE your big idea, the very next thing you should work on is your business plan. As we've seen, the business plan has several purposes. It captures your ideas on paper and keeps track of the steps you've taken or will take to start the business. It's also a major requirement in acquiring financing for your business. No one will want to help you start your business unless you can convince them that your plan will keep your business from crashing soon after takeoff.

Below, you will find a detailed guide for writing the sections that make up a basic business plan. We've written it with a funding request in mind; if you are creating your plan for your own reference, use your own judgment about the level of detail and items you include. Naturally, if you are writing your plan to test the idea of starting a certain business, you won't have any history to report either. It may help you to think of the project as writing several connected, self-contained reports.

* * *

The EXECUTIVE SUMMARY is the first part of a business plan and is the most crucial piece. It provides a very concise synopsis of the entire plan, along with a brief history of your company (if there is one). This portion tells readers what your business is or will be, and where you want to take it. It's the first thing your readers see; it will either grab their attention and make them want to keep learning, or make them want to close the cover and move on to something else. Most importantly, this part of the plan tells why you believe your business will be successful.

Here's a tip: The Executive Summary is most easily and effectively written after you finish writing the rest of your business plan. Once all of the details of your plan are in order, you will be prepared to condense it into the Executive Summary. Try to keep this section to fewer than four pages.

Included in the Executive Summary are:

- Mission Statement: The Mission Statement briefly explains the focus of your business. The statement can technically be any length, although we recommend shooting for two to three sentences. It should be as direct and concise as possible and it should leave the reader with a clear picture of what your business is all about.

- When the business was started

- Key management and their roles

- Number of employees

- Primary and other locations of the business

- Description of office, manufacturing plant, or facilities

- The products or services

- Current investor information and any additional financial relationships or arrangements

- Brief summary of your company's financial accomplishments and any noteworthy market activities (e.g., your business tripled its value in a one-year period or you became the leader in your industry by developing a certain product)

- Briefly describe management's plans for the business's future.

With the exception of the Mission Statement, the information in the Executive Summary should be presented in a brief or bulleted style. Note that this information is expanded upon in greater detail within the remainder of the business plan.

If you are just starting a business, you most likely will not have a lot of information to populate all the fields mentioned above. As an alternative, focus on your experience, background, and the decisions that led you to start the business. Ensure that it contains information about the needs your target market has and what solutions your business will provide. Explain how the business experience you have will allow you to make meaningful advances into the market. Point out what you're going to do uniquely or more effectively than your competition. Show that there is a definite need for the product or service provided by your business, then address the business's prospective plans.

To help the reader in pinpointing specific sections within your business plan, provide a table of contents immediately following the Executive Summary. The content titles should be very broad; try not to include too much detail.

* * *

The MARKET ANALYSIS portion is Part Two of a well-written business plan. It should demonstrate your knowledge of the particular industry that your business plans to enter. It should also provide basic statistics and key information of any market research data you have obtained. However, the itemized details of your market research studies should be placed in the Appendix section of the business plan.

This part of the business plan should include a description of the industry, target market facts and information, market test results, timeframes, and an evaluation of your competition.

The Industry Description section should include an overview of your primary industry: industry size, current and trailing growth rates, market trends and characteristics relating to the entire industry. What is the life-cycle stage of the industry? What is the industry's expected growth rate? It should profile the major customer groups within the industry (businesses, governments, women over 35 years of age, children under five, etc.). This can be broad or narrow, depending on the size and scope of the industry and the business you are in.

The business's target market is the customer base that it aims to supply products or provide services to. When defining a target market, it's vital to narrow the group to a realistic size. Often, businesses make the fatal miscalculation of trying to offer something to everybody. This approach typically ends in failure.

Within the Target Market section, you should report information that identifies the following:

- **Key characteristics** of the primary group you are targeting. This segment should include information about the critical needs of your future customers, the level to which those needs are currently being met, and the demographics of the group. Ensure you also include the geographic location of your target market; identify the key decision-makers, and any seasonal or cyclical trends that may impact the industry or your business model.

- **Size** of the target market. Here, you should report the number of potential customers in your primary market, the amount of annual purchases they make relative to products or services at par with your own, the geographic area they inhabit, and the expected market growth for this group.

- The **magnitude of market share** you expect to capture and the reasons why. When gathering this information, you need to decide how much market share and how many customers you expect to gain in a specific geographic region. In addition, you should provide the reader with an understanding of the reasoning you used in developing these estimates. Some businesses, for example day care centers, may be limited by law to the number of customers they can serve. Explain these things here if they apply.

- **Pricing and gross margin** expectations. In this section, it would be wise to define the structure of your pricing, your gross margin requirements, and any discounts or incentives that you plan to offer through the business, such as large-volume purchasing, bulk discounts, or prompt payment discounts that discourage customers from taking advantage of payment terms.

- A list of target market **research** and information sources. These resources can be purchased demographic research, directories, business associations, industry publications, and government documents. Or you can do your own digging.

- **Media** your business will use to reach the target audience. The media may include Internet marketing, Internet radio, conventional radio, trade shows, public speaking, networking, television, magazines, periodicals, flyers, or any other type of engaging media that has the potential to touch your target audience.

- **Buying patterns** of your target market. The first steps are to identify the needs of the potential consumers, conduct research in order to see how to address their needs, review the possibilities, and identify the person or persons that can put your offering in front of buyers.

- **Trends** that affect your potential customers, coupled with fundamental features of any secondary markets. As with the primary target market, it is important to pinpoint the needs, demographics and developing trends that are going to affect the secondary markets later.

Include information about any of the market tests already completed in this section. Specific details should be included in the Appendix. Market studies usually include the target customers who were contacted, all data or information that was provided to prospective customers, how critical satisfying their needs really is, and the target market's willingness to purchase products or services at a blend of different price-points from your business.

If appropriate, detail lead-time considerations. Lead-time is the required amount of time from when a customer places an order until the moment the product or service is delivered. When you research this information, determine your lead-times regarding initial orders, re-orders, and bulk purchases.

While conducting a competitive analysis (often called a SWOT Analysis— Strengths, Weaknesses, Opportunities and Threats), it is critical to identify the competition's product lines or services and market segment. Use this information to determine their strengths and weaknesses, understand the relationship between your target market and your competitors, and identify any opportunities and threats that may affect how you will enter the marketplace.

Also, be certain that you identify all of the primary competitors for each of the products or services offered. For each key competitor, determine their market share. Then try to predict when new competitors will enter into the marketplace. How long will your window of opportunity last? Finally, pinpoint any additional or less impactful competitors that may have an effect on your success. Your competitors' strengths or competitive advantages might become advantages that you too provide. These strengths can be found in many different areas of the business. They typically include:

- An ability to service customers' needs

- The ability to hold a great deal of market share (consumers' brand awareness comes with that)

- Years in business as a trusted organization

- Great financial position, ensuring that they can survive as a business through thick and thin

- Exceptional management or personnel

Weaknesses are easy to understand, as they are simply the opposite of strengths. However, it is important to analyze the same areas as you did for strengths, in order to determine the weaknesses of your competition. Do they satisfy the needs of their customers? What is their current market penetration? How well do the target audiences and the public view them in regard to past performance, trust, and reputability? Are they experiencing financial constraints or limitations? These could all be red flags for any business. If you discover weak spots in the competition, learn why these problems exist, so you can avoid them.

In the event that your target audience is not shared with your competition, you should be able to grow your idea with little resistance. However, if the competition is hungry for your target market, too, you should plan to handle the known roadblocks on your way to success. Some issues you may uncover include:

- High start-up costs

- Significant time required to get your idea off the ground

- Constantly evolving technologies

- Shortage of skilled personnel

- Customers unfamiliar with your company, product or service

- Current intellectual property laws such as patents and trademarks which may inhibit your ability to innovate

The last section that requires research here is the section covering restrictions and regulations. This includes information related to employees, customers, government regulations, and any other future changes. Important items that need to be addressed include steps necessary to conform to any current or pending requirements that affect your business, as well as the timeframe involved. When does your business have to be in compliance? On what date do these changes take effect? What resources do you need in order to conform?

* * *

The COMPANY DESCRIPTION is Part Three of your business plan. While keeping the finer details limited, provide the reader with a brief understanding of how all of the different components of your business work together. A company description typically provides information about the fundamentals of the business, along with a breakdown of the key factors that will lead to the business's success.

When providing the fundamentals of the business, it is important to include detail on the needs of the marketplace that you are trying to satisfy. Ensure you provide detail on the initiatives that you expect will satisfy these needs. Last, provide a breakdown of key individuals and major organizations that have these needs.

Fundamental factors of success typically include an ability to satisfy your customers' needs better than the competition, time- and cost-effective processes of providing products or services, valuable personnel, and quite often, a prime location. Any, or all, of these can be a competitive advantage.

* * *

The ORGANIZATION AND MANAGEMENT section is Part Four to a well-written business plan. This section provides profiles of key members of management. At a minimum, it should include an organization chart that shows the structure of the organization, profiles of key management and Board of Directors (if you have one), and other important ownership information.

The initial subsection of the Organization and Management portion of the business plan should describe structure of your organization. The most effective and cleanest way to show the company's structure is to provide readers with an organizational chart and narrative description. This will demonstrate to your readers that you leave nothing to chance, that a comprehensive plan is in place, and that the most appropriate employee is in charge of each function of the business. Drawing one up can sometimes reveal problems (like who reports to whom, or that one person in fact has two bosses) that you can address before they fester. Potential investors and employees alike find this very important.

Profiles of key management typically follow the organization's structure, listing each key member from top to bottom on your chart. What are the individual roles and responsibilities for members of management? What are their education and employment backgrounds and why are they being brought into the business as a member of the board or senior manager? These details may appear unnecessary in one- or two-person businesses; however, individuals, especially investors, reading the business plan, expect to know everyone's role and level of experience. Provide a well thought-out, detailed write-up, including the function of each department or facet of the business.

One of the most important components for success in the growth of any company is the ability and track record of its owner and management team. Let your readers know about the key people in your company and their backgrounds. Provide résumés that include the following information:

- Name
- Title (include a brief position description along with primary duties)
- Primary responsibilities and authority
- Education
- Unique experience and skills
- Prior employment
- Special skills
- Past track record

- Industry recognition

- Community involvement

- Number of years with the company

- Compensation basis and levels (if you are setting these for the first time, make sure these are reasonable—not too high or too low)

Ensure you quantify achievements (e.g., "Managed a sales force of ten people," "Managed a department of fifteen people," "Increased revenue by 15 percent in the first six months," "Expanded the retail outlets at the rate of two each year," "Improved the customer service as rated by our customers from a 60 percent to a 90 percent rating").

Also, highlight how the people surrounding you complement your own skills. If you're just starting out, show how each person's unique experience will contribute to the success of your venture.

While not all businesses have a Board of Directors, the major benefit of an unpaid advisory board is that it can provide expertise that your company cannot otherwise afford. A board composed of well-known, successful business owners or managers can go a long way toward enhancing your company's credibility and perception of management expertise.

If you have a Board of Directors, be sure to gather the following information when developing your business plan:

- Names

- Positions on the board

- Extent of involvement with the company

- Background

- Historical and future contribution to the company's success

Conclude this section by providing details regarding the legal structure of the business, followed by the ownership information. Is the business incorporated? What type of incorporation is it? Maybe you have an LLC or partnership. Or are you are set up as a sole proprietorship?

The following ownership information is important and necessary for the Organizational Structure section of a successful business plan:

- Owners' names

- Member interest breakdown (who owns how much)

- Company involvement

- Ownership types (such as common and preferred stock, general partner, limited partner)

- Any other existing equity equivalents such as warrants, options, convertible debt, etc.

- Common stock

* * *

The MARKETING AND SALES STRATEGIES section is Part Five of your business plan. Marketing is the process of creating customers, the lifeblood of your business. In this section, the first thing you want to do is define your marketing strategy. There is no single way to approach a marketing strategy. Your strategy should be part of an ongoing business-evaluation process and be unique to your company. However, there are common steps you can follow to help you think through the direction and tactics you would like to use to drive sales and sustain customer loyalty.

An overall marketing strategy should include, at a minimum, these four strategies:

- A market penetration strategy

- A growth strategy. This strategy for building your business might include an *internal* strategy such as how to increase your human resources, an *acquisition* strategy such as buying another business, a *franchise* strategy for branching out, a *horizontal* strategy where you would provide the same type of products to different users, or a *vertical* strategy where you would continue providing the same products but would offer them at different levels of the distribution chain.

- Channels of distribution strategy. Choices for distribution channels could include original equipment manufacturers (OEM's), an internal sales force, distributors, or retailers, licensees, and sister or daughter companies under a larger umbrella.

- Communication strategy. How are you going to reach your customers? Usually, a combination of the following tactics works the best: promotions, advertising, public relations, personal selling, and printed materials such as brochures, catalogs, flyers, etc.

After you have developed a comprehensive marketing strategy, you can then define your sales strategy. This covers how you plan to actually sell your products or services.

Your overall sales strategy should include two primary elements:

- A **sales force strategy**. If you are going to have a sales force, do you plan to use internal or independent representatives? How many salespeople will you recruit for your sales force? What type of recruitment strategies will you use? How will you train your sales force? What about compensation?

- Your **sales activities.** When you are defining your sales strategy, it is important that you break it down into activities. For instance, you need to identify your prospects. Once you have made a list of your prospects, you need to prioritize the contacts, selecting the leads with the highest potential to buy first. Next, identify the number of sales calls you will make over a certain period of time. From there, you need to determine the average number of sales calls you will need to make to win an order, the average sale per order, and the average sale per customer in a given period of time.

* * *

The SERVICE OR PRODUCT LINE section is Part Six of your business plan. What are you selling? In this section, describe your service or product, emphasizing the benefits to potential and current customers. For example, don't tell your readers which 89 foods you carry in your Gourmet-to-Go shop. Tell them why busy, two-career couples will prefer shopping in a service-oriented store that records clients' food preferences and caters to even the smallest parties on short notice.

Focus on the areas where you have a distinct advantage. Identify the problem in your target market for which your service or product provides a solution. Give the reader hard evidence that customers are, or will be, willing to pay for your solution. List your company's services and products and attach any marketing or promotional materials. Provide details regarding suppliers, availability of products or services, and product or service costs. Also include information addressing new products or services which will soon be added to the company's line.

This section should include:

- **A detailed description of your product or service** (from your customers' perspective). You should include information about the specific benefits of your product or service. You should also talk about your product or service's ability to meet consumer needs, or any advantages your offering has over the competition's.

- **Information related to your product's life cycle.** Include information about where your product or service is in its life cycle (e.g. idea, proto-type, etc.), as well as any factors that may influence its cycle in the future.

- Any **copyright, patent and trade secret information** that may be relevant. This should include information related to existing, pending or anticipated copyright and patent filings along with any key char-acteristics of your products or services for which you cannot obtain a copyright or patent. This is where you should also incorporate key aspects of your products or services that may be classified as trade se-crets (while not disclosing the secrets themselves). Last, but not least, be sure to add any information pertaining to existing legal agreements, such as nondisclosure or non-compete agreements.

- **Research and development (R&D) activities** you are involved in or are planning to be involved in, including any in-process or future activ-ities related to the development of new products or services. This sec-tion should also cover information about what you expect the results of future R&D activities to be. Be sure to analyze the R&D efforts of not only your own business, but also that of others in your industry.

* * *

The FUNDING REQUEST is Part Seven of your business plan, if that is your purpose for this version of your plan. In this section, you will request the amount of funding you will need to start or expand your business. If necessary, you can include different funding scenarios, such as best- and worst-case scenarios. Re-member that later, in the Financial section (see below), you must be able to back up these requests and scenarios with corresponding financial statements.

You will want to include the following in your funding request:

- Your **current** funding requirement

- Your **future** funding requirements over the next five years

- **How you will use** the funds you receive

- Any **long-range financial strategies** that you are planning that would impact your funding request

When you are outlining your current and future funding requirements, en-sure you include the amount you want now and the amount you want in the fu-ture, the time period that each request will cover, the type of funding you would like to have (e.g., equity, debt), and the terms that you would like to have applied.

How will you use your funds? This is very important to a creditor.

- Is the funding requested for capital expenditures (spending that creates future benefits, e.g., buying new kitchen equipment for your bakery business so that it can produce twice as many baked goods)?

- Is it for working capital (funding the general operations of your business)?

- Is it for debt retirement (paying off all or part of your business's debts)?

- Or acquisitions (purchasing new assets)?

Whatever it is, be sure to list it in this section.

Last of all, ensure that you include any strategic information related to your business that may impact your financial situation in the future, such as going public with your company, having a leveraged buyout, being acquired by another company. Explain the method by which you will service your debt, or whether or not you plan to sell your business in the future. Each of these is extremely important to a future creditor, since they will directly affect your ability to repay your loan(s) or influence the use of other funding.

* * *

The FINANCIALS section is Part Eight of your business plan. The financials should be developed after you've analyzed the market and set clear, realistic objectives. Only then can you allocate resources efficiently. The following is a list of the critical financial statements to include in your business plan packet:

Historical Financial Data. If you own an established business, you must supply historical data on your company's performance. Most creditors request data for the last three to five years, depending on the length of time you have been in business.

The historical financial data to include are your company's income statements (a list of sales, expenses, and profit for a given period), balance sheets (a summary of a business's financial condition, including assets, liabilities and net worth), and cash flow statements (statements, each for a given period, illustrating cash receipts and cash payments for a business) for each year you have been in business (usually for up to three to five years). Often, creditors are also interested in what collateral (personal assets pledged to secure a business loan) you may have, regardless of the stage of your business.

Prospective Financial Data. All businesses, whether start-up or growing, should supply prospective financial data. Most of the time, creditors will want to see what you expect your company to be able to do over the next five years. Each year's documents should include forecasted income statements, balance sheets, cash flow statements, and capital expenditure budgets (money spent to acquire or upgrade physical assets such as buildings and machinery). For the first year, you should supply monthly or quarterly projections. Thereafter, you can stretch it to quarterly and/or yearly projections for years two through five.

Ensure that your projections match your funding requests. Creditors are always on the lookout for inconsistencies. It's much better if you catch mistakes before they do. If you have made assumptions in your projections, be sure to summarize what you have assumed. This way, your reader will not be left guessing.

Finally, include a short analysis of your financial information. Include a ratio and trend analysis (compare the performance of different periods of time in order to highlight your business's growth) for all of your financial statements (both historical and prospective). Since pictures speak louder than words, you may want to add graphs of your trend analysis, especially if they are positive.

* * *

The APPENDIX, Part Nine, is the final section of your business plan. However, this section should be provided to readers only on an as-needed basis. In other words, it should *not* be included with the main body of your business plan. Your plan is your communication tool. As such, it will be seen by a lot of people. You will not want *everyone* to see some of the information in this section. Specific individuals (such as creditors) may want access to this information in order to make lending decisions. Therefore, it is important to keep it separate—yet to have the Appendix within easy reach.

The Appendix should include:

- Credit history (personal and business)

- Résumés of key managers

- Product pictures and other graphics

- Letters of reference

- Details of market studies

- Relevant magazine articles or book references

- Licenses, permits or patents

- Legal documents

- Copies of leases

- Building permits
- Contracts
- List of business consultants, including attorney and accountant

As we noted above, the distribution of your business plan should be controlled. Do ensure that you keep and maintain an accurate distribution record. This will allow you to update and maintain your business plan as needed. Also, ensure that you include a private placement disclaimer with your business plan if you plan to use it to raise capital (funding to run the operations of your business).

A.T.N.A. (All Talk, No Action)

*No one ever accomplished a goal by doing
a whole lot of nothing.*

HAVE YOU EVER, while sitting with friends or colleagues who are discussing a new business idea or job opportunity, said to yourself, "I've heard this record before"? Sure—we all have. It's a perfect example of the biggest bottleneck when it comes to achievement, productivity and success. Every time I hear someone say that they're "going to do" something, it's all I can do to not stand up on my chair and holler at them, "So, do it already!"

It's sad. So many people have genuinely great business ideas that, if implemented, could truly change their lives. Unfortunately most of them are too busy getting ready to get ready. You find them sitting in a coffee shop or a local watering hole, handing out their latest initiative's business cards and marketing materials while talking about how successful they will soon be. They proclaim that it's only going to take a few months of planning and execution before they get "there".

These people crack me up. They spend market launch money on screen-printed T-shirts, pens, magnets, and other corporate promotional material, in a sort of flavor-of-the-month approach. If they could simply stick with one thing for more than ten minutes, they would have something—something truly significant! The bottom line is the majority of businesses don't fail because of the product, service or idea, but because of the lack of dedication, follow-through and willingness to put rubber to the road.

Don't get caught in the loop. *Make it happen!*

Focus on reality instead of the loop. Although it is important to think through all of the risks of a venture, it is equally important to revisit the idea or widget that got you excited in the first place, zoom up to take an aerial view, and recognize that you may be over-thinking the details. Don't be afraid to go back to basics, especially if it helps reconfirm the viability of your whole idea.

I'm the first to admit that I've been there. I'm the guy who used to analyze everything to the most microscopic detail, trying to find the flaws, when in reality, what I was focusing on was so far away from the main idea that days, weeks and months would fly by. By the time I came up for air, I was so burned out that I wasn't even interested any more. Nor did I think the idea would work.

I'm not saying the details aren't important. I'm simply saying that sometimes you need to focus on the whole plate, not each individual pea. Don't be afraid of taking the first step toward your goal.

M.O.

Prioritizing Your Way to Success*

Don't get out too far over your skis, unless you want to slide down the mountain on your face. Here are some helpful tips.

EVERYBODY PLANS—it's a part of our lives, and human nature. When you go to the grocery store, you make a list. The question now is: How long does it take you to do it your shopping?

Do you spend an hour in the grocery store because you go down the list from top to bottom, ignoring the order of your groceries' placement in the store? Or do you shop smart, bring a pencil, and go from one side of the store to the other, checking your items off the list as you go? (Or for the ultimate list-maker, do you organize your shopping list to match the store's layout?)

Shopping habits aside, let's apply the scenario to the working world. With today's economy, chances are that if you have a job, you're probably overworked and never feel like you've completed all your tasks. If you're an entrepreneur trying to start your own business, you see an endless list of tasks to do, in order to get your operation off the ground or grown to the next level. Have you finished writing your business plan? Have you researched funding options? Have you planned how you're going to go public? Do you have enough employees or farmed-out resources to get you off the ground and up to a competitive momentum?

If you answered 'yes' to *all* of those questions, I'm afraid that you're not using your time as wisely as you could. The one you should have left alone was the plan for going public. If you're just trying to start a small business and are wasting time thinking about going public, it means that you're not focusing enough on what you should be focusing on: the Now. It takes years for the average privately owned company to go public or release their initial public offering (IPO).

*If you're a fan of 1950's dramatic theater, the "or" title to this section would be, "The Case of the Entrepreneur Who Spread Himself Too Thin and Accomplished Nothing".

The reason why may not be why you think. Think about it from an investor's standpoint. Would you give a huge amount of money to a company that had only had its doors open for five minutes? I know I wouldn't—out of principle. Successful investors didn't get to be investors because they were naïve or stupid.

So if you're focusing on tasks that don't need pondering for another five years, then you're not getting done now what needs to happen to get you to that five-year point. We call it "getting out over your skis". If you're whipping down a steep slope and lean too far forward, you're going to end up flat on your face in the snow.

The solution is to stick to the Now and prioritize. If you need to make a gigantic list (as I often do), then do so. After I've made my list, I often sub-categorize my list in order to break it into major (often profit-bearing) accomplishments, and the tasks that each requires. That way, I can focus on one project and ensure that I accomplish everything I need in order to make that initiative profitable.

S.G.

The Importance of Market Testing

Would you dive into a body of water if you couldn't see below the surface? The same concept applies to entrepreneurs and market testing.

MY WIFE HAS a burning desire to open a bakery in our community. She watched one of those reality shows about an independently owned bakery and saw how much fun it was for a couple of sisters (she has two) to own a bakery together. She loved how popular the bakery was, how much money the sisters made, and how all the beautiful people were flowing in and out of the bakery all day long. In the episode that I watched for five minutes, it really looked like heaven on earth for those reality TV sisters and their glorious bakery.

In support of my wife, I will admit that she creates the most delicious cakes and treats that I have ever tasted, and I'm a pretty well-travelled (and well-fed) guy. My wife's culinary skills are unquestionably a very marketable product. It wasn't her skills, however, that were blocking my full support of this endeavor.

We live in a relatively small town, about thirty minutes away from the nearest big city. There aren't a lot of foot-traffic areas, and aside from a few small, wealthy neighborhoods, the average state of wealth isn't very high. While our community is by no means impoverished, it's just not fancy. After she mentioned that she wanted to open a small bakery, I spent some time on Google and looked up every small bakery in our area. I spent a couple hours driving by every one and checking out their operations. In the end, I wasn't convinced that an independent bakery was the wisest endeavor. While the bakeries weren't shabby, they didn't look profitable, either.

Not quite ready to give up on my wife's dream, I went home to consult with my old friend, Google, again. This time, I looked up the tax information in public records of each of the bakeries, as well as the average cost of rent and purchase for retail space with existing functional, installed kitchen equipment, in our area.

While the claimed income for the bakeries (from the tax info) was more than I expected it would be, it was the cost of the real estate that blew me away.

While a privately owned bakery *could* be profitable, the residents in our community couldn't afford what my wife and her sisters would have to charge for their treats to be able to keep the bakery's doors open for business. Expensive cupcakes might fly in the "big city," but they don't in my humble community, where the majority of its citizens are on retiree fixed budgets.

The fact is that desserts are a luxury. They could be the most delicious desserts in the world, but if people can't afford to pay what they must cost, there isn't much else anyone can do.

Ideas for making this work, however, include catering and/or delivery to neighboring communities (to broaden your customer base) or perhaps even international dry-ice shipping (to broaden your customer base even more).

The moral of the story is that even great business ideas and stellar products don't work everywhere. Too often, entrepreneurs spend too much time focusing on their supply, and not enough on the demand. In short, if no one's there to buy, you won't be selling anything. I'm not trying to crush anyone's dreams here. I just suggest that you do your due diligence before you launch an endeavor. Research what *your* market will bear.

S.G.

The Four Worst Entrepreneurial Mistakes

Get right what so many others get wrong.

HERE ARE THE FOUR WORST THINGS entrepreneurs do as they start businesses.

Thinking that you can do it all and accomplish your goals without help. Just because you might be starting a business alone doesn't mean that you won't need help. Success depends on developing and using a network of colleagues, friends, mentors and professionals that can provide advice, assistance and direction in tough times. This applies in particular to getting help from lawyers and accountants. With the vast potential for error in the legal and bookkeeping arenas of business start-ups, they more than pay for themselves as preventive maintenance.

Thinking for one second that you don't need a business plan. It's a fact that there is a direct correlation between planning and success. By failing to plan, you are planning to fail. Some foolish entrepreneurs think that they can coast through the planning process and just make wordsmithing adjustments to their plans as they go along. Others have the foolish misconception that a business plan would limit their creativity or spontaneity. Still others feel that their business isn't large enough or complex enough to warrant a plan. Here's the deal: every business can benefit from a business plan, no matter what size it is. The process of developing a business plan crystalizes your strategy and helps you chart your priorities.

Assuming that you'll make it big quickly or easily. I'll be honest with you. When you're starting a business, there's good news and bad news. The good news is that by starting a business, you'll get to live out your dreams; the bad news is that no matter what you do, it's never as easy as you think it will be. There are a lot of assumptions tied up with the practice of starting a business. The reality is that success takes very long hours, strategic planning, and a diehard commitment to the legwork involved. While the result can be wonderful, once the work is done, the work is never as easy as you think it will be.

Not conducting a market test or doing research. Just because you have a great idea doesn't mean you have a business. As we've seen, the most common question among would-be entrepreneurs after conceptualizing a new idea is "Now what?" Just because you've thought of a great concept or idea doesn't mean that the Great Idea Fairy is going to visit you in the night and give you a wheelbarrow filled with cash. Patenting, trademarking or copyrighting your great idea is a good start—right before you start writing your business plan.

CHAPTER II

Getting Financed

How to Obtain Business Financing

*Unless your new business is a money-tree farm, you
will find this chapter very useful.*

THERE ARE MANY DIFFERENT ways to acquire financing, so preparation
and research will pay off well for you. Before searching for financing, it is a good
idea to see what grants and subsidies you might qualify for. They could keep you
from incurring debt or losing ownership. However, if you don't find such funding
available, a variety other sources of financing can help you get your new business
off the ground.

When determining what type of financing to procure for your business,
there are many avenues to consider. Depending on the type of business you have,
your future plans, and the product(s) and service(s) you offer, the choice is important. There are two main types of financing: debt or equity. *Debt financing* is the
process by which a firm borrows capital from banks and investors, promising to
repay the borrowed funds within a certain amount of time or incur some type of
liability, usually in the form of interest. The other type is *equity financing,* when an
organization relinquishes ownership interest to different sources in exchange for
capital. Most well-capitalized businesses use a balance of both. This helps mitigate
risk and keep the cost of capital to a minimum.

Debt financing is usually done by businesses that have either established
positive cash flow (money remaining after collecting rent and paying operating expenses and mortgage payments) or have the necessary collateral (equipment, cash
or an individual's promissory note) to secure the funds from a lender. When businesses choose this method, they are obliged to pay a carrying cost on the funds.
This is common among two types of businesses. One type deals in high-volume
inventory purchases that are later liquidated through sales channels, thus keeping
the term of the loan to a minimum. The other type needs to expand by purchasing
space or equipment with a liquidation value similar to the debt outstanding (real
estate, long-term-use equipment, and vehicles).

Another approach is equity financing. It can be a great tool when expanding your firm beyond the size and scope of what you could fund with conventional debt financing. In equity financing, you effectively sell an interest in your company in exchange for funding provided by a partner or investor. That way, you can raise needed capital, while only being exposed to a few key liabilities like rent or mortgage, equipment expenses, and employee salaries.

In order to avoid takeovers or buyouts by these parties, you need to consider who holds the controlling interest in an equity deal. Whoever owns more than 50 percent, the majority percentage of the company's shares, gets to call the shots. Also, depending on the way in which the interest is conveyed, individuals can recoup their investment through multiple channels. This is when contracts detailing cash capital disbursements (debt repayment and/or interest payment) are important.

Here's an example of a vital cash capital disbursement decision. Imagine you accepted a large start-up loan from an investor to get your business off the ground. What does your cash capital disbursement contract say about your repayment terms? Specifically, when you have to pay it back? Do you have to start repaying the loan immediately, or after three to five years? It makes a pretty big difference.

If you have to start paying back the loan immediately, the principal (original amount) plus interest will put a pretty big dent in your allocated operating budget, from Day One. Is the loan even worth it, at this point? You can see why your cash capital disbursement terms are extremely important. Make sure the financial terms to which you agree are feasible for you.

Lastly, remember that there is a strong correlation between risk and reward in funding. If you have to relinquish a good portion of your ownership interest to other investors in order to get the money you need, you may only be entitled to a small portion of the profits, in the event that the business performs extremely well.

There are many different types of private investors and investment groups. The most common is the *accredited investor*. These individuals are familiar with the investment world and have probably participated in such ventures previously. They also have certain qualifications to make them attractive financiers. Another type is an *angel investor*, an individual who has the funds to almost entirely fund the start-up, expansion or growth of a business. Both accredited investors and angel investors are private parties who are not usually affiliated with an investment group.

Investment groups, such as *venture capitalists* (VC's), are another option. Venture capital groups are great for companies that are interested in retaining brain-trust equity and/or a portion of the control, but not all. These groups tend to know exactly what they are looking for in exchange for their involvement. The right to controlling interest and substantial portions of revenue is not uncommon. However, by using such groups, a business's current owners can nearly eliminate their personal financial risk. Because the VCs have a sizeable vested interest, expect the participation of seasoned business consultants who will take a hands-on approach and work with your firm to achieve success.

Some businesses have the ability to approach the public through an *initial public offering* (IPO). This is the process by which a company works with investment bankers to build a following in a specific trading platform (e.g., a stock exchange), then offers shares representing interest in the company on its behalf, in exchange for a portion of the proceeds. Usually a company has to have a proven track record to launch an IPO, so don't waste time dreaming about IPOs in your early start-up days unless others with experience confirm it's worth considering.

There can be great benefits as well as detriments associated with making an initial public offering. The most common advantage is that, on average, a firm can collect ten times its value in one offering. In special circumstances, when either the product or service is groundbreaking or there is a large emotional following in the market, an organization can raise exponentially more. This happened frequently during the dot-com era, in the late Nineties, when technology companies were making IPOs and the stock prices were driven up to staggering multiples above book value, simply because of investors' speculation on the potential for future success.

Local, regional, or even national governments often provide funding for entrepreneurs, as the Small Business Administration (SBA) does in the US. Especially for new businesses, the SBA offers competitive loans, grants and subsidies. However, the majority of these funds are only released to businesses or individuals with specific profiles, such as minorities, persons with disabilities, and individuals coming from a disadvantaged socioeconomic background. If you qualify for this avenue for funding, you will encounter numerous waiting periods that can only be expedited by spending more money. Most of the forms necessary for different filings can be filled out digitally and submitted online, or they can be downloaded, printed and then faxed to the necessary recipient.

If you are based in a location where special business development incentives are available, be sure to check them out. Has your area suffered from had a natural disaster, so that funds are now available to recover and start new businesses? Do your local or higher levels of government, or your industry sector, award grants or subsidies to encourage companies to open new markets, employ certain kinds of workers, or develop products or services in line with governmental planning goals?

With all these sources of money, be careful to not get ahead of yourself. If your regional government offers to pay for companies to attend trade fairs in new markets, for example, don't go first and apply for reimbursement later. You will often find these aids need to be applied for and approved before the action they encourage gets started. Still, they are a great boon for start-ups and expanding businesses.

The Transformation of Lending

As the access door to lending closes, small businesses
are seeking capital elsewhere. Here's why.

ONE OF THE SINGLE greatest frustrations for small businesses is limited access to capital. A few years ago, entrepreneurs could approach traditional banks with business plans, projections, plus a good credit history, and secure reasonable financing under favorable terms. Today, the requirements for underwriting a loan are so difficult that conventional bank lending is limited to a much smaller percentage of qualified applicants. This reality is causing a shift in the lending environment. In this section and the next, we'll map the emerging terrain.

Traditional banks are beginning to see loan requests diminish, as entrepreneurs and small businesses pursue alternate sources for capital. One emerging source is private placement capital from individuals who prefer to loan capital to small businesses at higher interest rates than they have been receiving from bank deposit accounts or investment accounts. With the proper presentation and disclosure of the small business's performance and opportunity, a private individual often finds the premium interest rate provided by the small business a welcome change from traditional alternatives. In some cases, these lending programs can grow into opportunities for permanent investment into the small business. Banks meanwhile are diminishing their lending portfolio while seeing drops in certain customers' deposit accounts, as these investors take out money to privately fund small business loans.

The larger scale opportunity for funding is with venture capital resources that often search for emerging businesses that present an opportunity for a substantial return in a specific time frame. They are often interested in a 20 percent annual return on their investment. This means that either through interest, dividend or equity sale, they like to fund a program where they can see substantial financial results in three to seven years. The key to using these sources is related to the strength of the financial opportunity if these funds are provided. Rapid growth models with large payoffs upon execution are typical for these sources of capital.

In between the large venture capital source and the individual private investor you can find angel investors. These sources often consider providing mid-range amounts and have more flexibility in how they approach an investment. There may be broader options for length of term, method of return, elements of equity, and other variables to a deal.

The common element that seems to be present in more popular lending sources for small businesses and entrepreneurs is a greater focus and weight on the *prospective* elements of the opportunity than the *retrospective* results of the business. In traditional bank lending, the focus is clearly on the past financial performance, supported by business and personal creditworthiness. Prospective elements of the opportunity are simply an accent to the process and of very little importance in the loan underwriting by traditional bank lending.

With traditional bank lending fixated on historical business results, it is not surprising that forward-looking entrepreneurs are turning away from traditional banks. As these newer lending resources become the basis for small business funding, we expect traditional banking will continue to erode, causing a transformation of lending, the world over.

Building a Financial Foundation for Your Business

When seeking financial backing from an outside source, ask yourself: Which is best for my company?

AS WE HAVE SEEN, THERE are many different methods of obtaining financing for your business. Even if your start-up is so small that you don't need any initial outside investment, I still encourage you to read on. If your business thrives, there's always the chance you'll need expansion capital at some point down the road.

You can get financing from a venture capital group, angel investors, the bank, or even a family members or friends. You have to find out the eligibility requirements of each of the four sources so you can determine which form of financing is best suited for your company.

Venture capital groups, angel investors, and bank financing can help a business get started and increase momentum without the risk of putting personal relationships and money in jeopardy. Let's look a little closer at how they operate.

Venture capital groups (VCs) are organizations that normally invest capital in an already operating business. They alleviate risk by investing in companies that are already financially stable. Typically, they offer short-term investments for up to five years. Unlike other investors, venture capitalists only expect returns on their investments, and have little or no interest in co-owning the businesses they invest in.

You should rule out venture capitalists if you are just starting out or are still in the conceptual stages, because they probably will do the same to you. If you still want to give them a try, be prepared. They will expect you to deliver a fully developed business plan and financials as well, including a report on how you managed your finances over the past three to five years. If they are interested in your venture, they will assign an employee in their company to analyze and evaluate everything that your company has done and will do in the foreseeable future, to protect their investment and be aware of daily operations.

If your new business and doesn't have three to five years of history yet, you still have a chance of getting the amount you desire from an **angel investor**. An angel investor (also known as a *business angel* or *informal investor*) is an individual who provides capital for business start-ups, usually in exchange for convertible debt (debt that can be converted to a specified related security if the parties agree) or ownership equity. Increasingly, angel investors are organizing themselves into angel groups or angel networks to share research, pool their investing funds, and spread the risks among a number of ventures. These investors normally invest in new businesses that look particularly promising.

Angel investors, whether individuals or organizations, may ask for their returns on investment in cash, or alternatively, ask to be co-owners of the business. Angel investors make long-term investments, unlike the venture capital groups. The investment amount may range from thousands to hundreds of thousands, or even millions of dollars, depending on the kind of investor(s) that you approach.

Locating the proper VC firm or angel investor for your initiative is a crucial step as well. How do you know which one is right for you? For the most part, simple research is vital. Basic Internet searches of the most reputable firms can reveal information on their reputation, previous and current project activity, and areas of expertise. You can find additional information by visiting a firm's website and requesting references, and even by inquiring with legal and accounting firms specializing in the industry specific to your project.

Note that most VC firms and angel organizations specialize in certain industry sectors, such as technology, health care, financial services, and even government contracts. Some investors even prefer investing in a certain geographic region; others have strict criteria for the actual monetary amount they tend to invest. It is important to focus your research by identifying those firms that are most closely related to your investment needs. This process has no timetable, so allow the maximum time possible to ensure your plan is presented to the firm(s) with the highest probability of investment funding, well ahead of the date you need a decision. A sloppy, urgent, or hastily prepared proposal can spoil your chance of future funding, so get everything as right as you can the first time.

Of course, you can also acquire **bank financing** for your business. If you have a business that has been operating for a period of time, this is another good option. The bank will consider your financial statements and credit history before it grants you a loan. Sometimes, they may elect to give you a smaller loan than you had first requested, depending on your financial status and the bank policies, to test how well you perform as a creditor. When you are applying for a bank loan, evaluate all the terms, including interest rates and re-payment periods. Always remember to read the fine print. Different banks have varying interest rates, so make sure to balance the best rates with your ability to pay back the loan in a short period of time. Be sure you understand a bank's policy on prepayment penalties (a fee for paying a loan off early), if applicable.

Some banks do not offer loans to start-ups, because they consider these loans to be high risk, with a high probability of having difficulties when it comes time to pay the loan back. However, if you provide collateral for the loan, the bank may be more favorable. Some of the collateral that you can provide includes business assets, title deeds, car logbooks, and other items with concrete value. Keep in mind, though, that if you fail to repay the loan, you will lose whatever you provided as collateral.

When researching bank financing options, one solution may be to seek financing from multiple bank sources, if that is permitted by all the lending parties. Although it still represents the same money coming to you, this approach lessens the risk for each lender (and perhaps gives you more control and flexibility). Separate lines of credit in various forms can also be an option, depending on the type of financing, loan amount, and/or collateralization you seek. Take care not to commit the same collateral to two parties!

If you feel that you are able to work with your **friends and family**, and they have resources and interest in financing your business, you should consider this. Working with them can be rewarding and challenging at the same time. It's sometimes hard to mix business with your personal life, but if you can persuade your circle to advance you a loan at a better rate than the banks, then you will save the accumulated interest. (And you never know, they might not charge you any interest at all.)

If you get financing this way, whether or not your friends and family do choose to charge you interest, use written financing agreements just as you would with any other investor, and outline the payment terms and interest rate everyone has agreed to. Also, make sure everybody understands all terms of the contract so there won't be a discrepancy that causes tension later.

For the loan period, be sure to keep your investors up on how your business is doing, informally or formally. If you run into financial problems with your company, your chances are much higher to being able to re-negotiate the terms of your loan to save your business with family members and friends than with a bank or VC group. But for all lenders, if troubles come as a surprise, it's natural that they could be worried about their current investment and be reluctant to help further in the future.

As you start and grow your company, you may find that first personal, then bank or angel, and finally venture capital and IPO financiers will work best for you. The secret is to carefully evaluate what's best today, so you can get to the next level tomorrow.

Getting Your Business the Credit It Deserves

Your business's credit score is like your business's financial reputation and bargaining power. Take care of it and it will take care of you.

CREDIT IS THE MEASURE that lenders use to gauge whether your small business qualifies for a loan, as well as the loan amount (sorry, you might not get the amount you want simply because you've been approved). There are numerous credit scoring models being used for various purposes around the world.

In the United States, for example, the most recognized and commonly-used system is known as FICO, named for the Fair Isaac Corporation. It is used to determine credit scoring in order to evaluate whether an individual is eligible for a loan or an extension of additional credit. The scoring system, used by the three largest credit reporting agencies in the US, allocates a number, ranging from 300 (extremely poor credit risk) to 900 (ranked perfect credit). The current average credit score in the US, as determined by Experian, Equifax and Trans Union, is approximately 692. Your FICO score is based on five factors: amount owed, payment history, span of credit history, new credit, and the various types of credit used.

A number of factors come into play when you think about obtaining credit (or even initial financing) for your small business. If the credit you are seeking is for a new business, your business-to-be will have no credit history or track record in the industry. Therefore, your personal credit report and score will most likely be used to determine the creditworthiness of your business. It can be difficult for an individual to get a loan while facing personal debts, and in certain circumstances, even applying for a loan can be damaging to your credit score. One way to make an improvement to your credit score is by improving your debt-to-income ratio. That means that paying off debts or loans can improve your credit score.

Once a business has been successfully launched, the new entity can begin establishing its own identity regarding good fiscal responsibility. Smart accounting practices and solid record keeping, combined with tangible evidence of successful dealings with vendors, employees and creditors over time, pave the way for the foundation of your business's own solid credit history and creditworthiness. This activity is captured and archived by the rating agencies in the same way personal credit is established, and thus a business credit report is created.

Business credit reports and business credit scores are calculated independently from your personal credit report and personal credit scores. Although it draws on the same types of information and data as a personal credit report, a business credit report is specific to a business's debt service, tax liens and/or public records. Business credit scores may be comprised of information regarding the owners of the business and possibly its officers. Often they are examined by creditors in combination with personal credit reports for a small business owner seeking financing.

Around the world, credit reports and scores do not intermix. For example, an American credit score is not transferable into Europe. Additionally, credit scores do not transfer from one European country to another. As a result, if you (or your business) relocate globally, a new credit history will probably have to be built up. However, a credit score in most parts of Europe is usually factored similarly to an American credit score. Factors such as public records, negative reports, late payments, and revolving and installment credit accounts are captured and archived. So, it's safe to say that wherever you are based, in order to develop and subsequently sustain a good credit standing and a high credit score, it is vital to uphold a satisfactory repayment history and debt-to-income ratio. While each country's specific credit reporting and collecting practices may differ, accounts in good standing will be required.

For any business to succeed, good credit control practices and solid record keeping are essential. This is particularly true for a small business. A high number of small businesses end up being declared bankrupt each year because of inadequacies in these areas.

Another reason why credit control is so imperative is that new small businesses may find it difficult to establish lines of credit with suppliers. Most suppliers expect a small business to make consistent, on-time payments (even, in some cases, pre-payments) for the goods and services purchased. Good credit, coupled with a high credit score, helps you get favorable conditions on business loans, insurance premiums, lease payments, and interest rates, all of which impact your cash flow.

So that's why a good credit score forms the financial foundation of every small or new business. It puts the organization in a position to acquire funding for capital expenditures, expansion, employment creation, research, and future development. It remains a key factor in the growth of any business and guarantees a promising future.

And there's an added benefit. Maintaining a good score allows a business owner to closely monitor cash, thus ensuring that the cost of running a business doesn't become a problem. This kind of liquidity allows you to respond promptly to time-sensitive money needs without compromising processes. Specialized credit and financial advisers can offer guidance for establishing, monitoring, improving and protecting your all-important credit rating.

CHAPTER III

Getting Started

Stage of Business Balanced with Speed of Business

Finding the perfect cross between planning and execution just got easier.

ONE OF THE MORE difficult challenges facing businesses today is determining the best balance between preparation and execution of a project or program. Too often, we drag out the preparation of an important initiative, beyond the critical window of time for action, and we find suddenly it's too late to act. Alternatively, we may jump too fast into execution and neglect vital preparations, failing to achieve the objective for a different reason. What is the correct balance between preparation and execution?

The secret to balance lies in the understanding of the current stage of your business's development. Key stages are these:

- *Start-up,* when the business is initially being organized and launched;

- *Development,* when the business is focused on a steady growth plan from its starting size to a target operating level;

- *Maintenance,* when the business reaches a relative plateau in size and scale;

- *Decline,* when the business is shrinking steadily due to a number of possible circumstances; and

- *Turn-Around,* when a business goes through a significant reorganization to create fresh momentum, emerging to look much like a start-up business.

When we think of preparation, we picture research, planning, setting processes and schedules, lining up resources, making choices of vendors or sellers, and so on. Execution is show-time: Everything you planned gets moving.

Start-up businesses are just getting started, and need to move from zero revenue to an acceptable level of revenue in an expected period of time to achieve a financially sustainable position. They need to over-execute, even at the risk of limited preparation. Preparation, however, should never be ignored or slighted in the process. Execution is the critical variable that leads to growth.

As you progress from Start-up to Development, you organize a plan of action and proceed down a path that may require continuous adjustment until you achieve the necessary outcomes and momentum. It can be frustrating if you need to adjust more times than anticipated, and if you expend more capital than planned. But it's just a fact that lots of execution may be required in the Development stage of a business. As Thomas Edison said, "I have learned over a hundred ways how not to make a light bulb."

Knowing that for most entrepreneurs, capital is limited, it is critical to execute at a pace that reaches a positive outcome before your capital is depleted. In other words, you need to start bringing in new money before you run out of your seed money. You may need to limit the time you spend in preparation, in order to execute more initiatives that will pay off soon, given your limited time and capital. In Start-up, you acquire significant knowledge by taking action. Losing small battles and learning from them often wins the war. The key is to learn and adjust, not make the same mistakes repeatedly. Small degrees of preparation shortfalls are more than offset by your ability to execute more initiatives. In Development, your focus is more on learning from earlier mistakes, and smoothing things out so you can deliver reliable results.

As a business matures and becomes more established, the Maintenance cycle of business kicks in. It brings a different perspective. With age comes a new element: experience. You will have more accumulated knowledge from the Development cycle. You may have more established components in your business, ones that would be negatively impacted by any preparation errors with new initiatives. You have more established customers and programs that might be jeopardized by an initiative that is poorly conceived. Therefore, in more established and mature businesses, it is important to be thorough in your preparation process and understand all the complex impacts to your entire existing business model.

The larger danger in Maintenance is to get so deep into the preparation process that the execution never happens. To avoid this, it is imperative to build project timelines that define each step of the preparation process and pair it with a clear deliverable by a specific deadline. Then, at each scheduled deadline, you can assess the continuing viability of an initiative and determine if you will amend the plan, abandon it, or continue toward the next step and possible execution.

Compartmentalization in this stage allows for close examination of each facet, in order to more easily identify issues. But the task of identifying an issue is much more daunting if a company has developed a complex structure (and even more so if it suffers from "silos"). In more established businesses, this process often moves more slowly because the urgency felt in a start-up or developing business has been replaced with a greater tolerance for planning, meeting, discussing and debating to protect the success of the existing core business. The key here is to accept the nature of a more elaborate preparation process, but manage it to execution with a clear timeline management process.

Businesses that have become complacent and have failed to adjust or change to maintain their success often move into a Declining cycle of business. They fail to identify and react to changes in the business environment, new competition or technologies, or various aspects of their market. The Decline cycle can kill a company, but if its leaders wake up in time, they may be able to make the necessary changes that threaten its extinction. In short, they stop the problem from getting worse, then solve it. The challenge in this cycle of business is that the existing management often has difficulty seeing beyond the symptoms of the decline and misses the actual root causes. Egos, corporate politics, and ingrained habits make fundamental change difficult to execute. This is a time when very candid and thorough analysis and planning is the most critical to determine root causes. Often, outside resources with a fresh perspective are needed to stop the decline and reestablish growth.

If the business is able to reestablish momentum, adapt to new circumstances, or a radical change occurs with ownership and/or management that implements an effective reorganization plan, the business moves into the Turn-Around cycle. It begins to act a bit like a start-up, developing business that is focused on rapid growth and momentum. In the Turn-Around cycle of business, leadership must act decisively to create the necessary reversal of momentum from Declining and launch a fresh new growth cycle for the business.

The point to remember, regardless of the current cycle of your business, is that the speed of business is always relative to your stage of business. If you are struggling to achieve momentum as a start-up, you need to push the envelope on rapid execution, accepting some measured and limited risk in the preparation process. It's all about moving, taking action, and adjusting along the way until you reach a financially sustainable level. In a more established business stage, you need to protect the core model while you execute new initiatives. A slower pace of execution is acceptable to protect the impact to the core business, but don't let yourself get caught in a failure to execute. A project timeline will help keep the process on track and focused on a conclusion, saving it from slipping into Decline and setting it on a negative course. The key is to pay attention to the cycle of your business now, to know where you are headed, and to respond appropriately to the speed of business to meet or exceed your goals for success.

How to Blue Chip Your Business

When you're just starting out with a new business, you probably lie awake at night wondering if you're making the most of your resources and opportunities. Rest easy with these brilliant options for catapulting your new business to the next level—overnight.

IN THE BEGINNING, every small business struggles to look like a solid, reputable company. The appearance of stable success helps generate more business by increasing your credibility and trust in the eyes of your customers. Most of all, it helps small businesses interact with larger players within their industry. Working on a limited budget? Don't lose hope; there are a few easy steps you can take to immediately make your business look solid, successful and professional for little or no cost.

A good first step is to go to a mailbox shop. You'll find Mail Boxes Etc. shops in the UK, South Africa or Australia; or a UPS Store in the US. Pick one that is located in an area of town or a specific city that has the feel you would like to have for your business address. Set up a mailbox with them, in your business's name. If it happens to be hard to get there, simply set up mail forwarding to your actual address.

It is important to seek out one of these stores because they accept mail and packages from all carriers, unlike certain government mail carriers, such as the US post office. Also, remember that if you get a PO Box from a particular mail carrier, you will have a PO Box address, which isn't professional-looking at all. If anything, it looks shady and makes people doubt the legitimacy of your business, which is exactly opposite what you want. How would you like to do business with an organization that advertises its storefront as a tiny metal box?

Most mailboxes set up through either Mail Boxes Etc. or UPS Stores allow the box owners to use the physical address of the store, followed by the mailbox number written as a suite (#), just the same as if it were a suite in an office building. Most people assume that an office suite is a Class A office space in a nice part of town. See, you're moving up already!

Another smart move is to setup a VOIP or "Voice-Over Internet Protocol" number. These toll-free numbers are great because they are very inexpensive and add another professional component to a small business. Most people associate toll-free numbers with larger firms and Fortune 500 companies. Now, with a VOIP number, individuals and small businesses can have toll-free numbers at very low rates. For example, a small business in the US could have a VOIP number for as little as $9.99 a month through companies like Ring Central.

Virtual Receptionists are the next step to polishing your phone presence. Most voice-over (VO) specialists charge about US$125 or £80 for every 75 words they record as your answering message. You can hire either a man or a woman, from anywhere in the world, depending on what type of voice you would like answering calls for your business. With a foreign language via a multi-lingual taped greeting or high prestige-accented voice, you've just added an international component to your business. These pre-recorded answering messages can be coupled with interactive response systems that allow callers to enter an extension or to select departments from a menu, such as "For sales, press 1; for customer support, press 2," etc. Think twice before you make people go through these mazes, however, as they are not callers' favorite use of time. And if it's early days in your business and all the calls come to you anyway, it's best to wait.

If you already have a website, fantastic! You'll be able to take advantage of this tip, which is the opposite from our advice above about telephone extensions. Set up contact emails for individual departments or services within your small business. Don't worry about the size of your small business or how many email accounts you set up. This helps give the appearance of a large, efficient, well-organized company. Best of all, you can forward all of the email addresses into one central account that you can easily check by yourself. For example, sales@ yourwebsite.com, support@yourwebsite.com, HR@yourwebsite.com, admin@ yourwebsite.com, etc. are all possible. The list can go on and on. Just be realistic and think about what makes the most sense for you and your business.

Don't forget about incubator office spaces or suites. These types of offices exist all over the world and allow individuals and start-up businesses to lease small office spaces (sometimes, even with light manufacturing space) within larger, typically full-service facilities, such as a Class-A space in a downtown or city center. You can even rent a fully-equipped boardroom with projectors, videocam set-ups and such for a few hours. These incubator communities can be invaluable because of the low set-up costs, the opportunity for you to have ongoing interaction with other entrepreneurs, and the availability of boardrooms, receptionists and more expensive office equipment that otherwise isn't affordable a small start-up company or home office.

In about five minutes, you've learned how to place your business anywhere you want it, add international cachet, and bring in big-business functions, all for extremely low costs that are kind to your growing small business. Work smarter, not harder!

Designing a Logo to Establish Your Brand and Image

While you might be creative, it's best to leave this one to professionals.

IN THE STIFF COMPETITION businesses face today, every marketer struggles to achieve or maintain success. Corporate logos are used as attention-grabbing identities in the marketplace. A logo positions a business and helps distinguish it from its competition. Therefore, it's worth taking time, money and attention to get your logo right. It can be a lot of fun!

There are many ways to design a corporate logo. The Internet gives a range of templates and can help a great deal in developing an attractive logo. Another option is hiring a logo designer to do it. You don't necessarily have to spend a lot of money on this; talented freelance artists are widely available for this work. Check their portfolios and get references and job quotes before signing up. Of course, there are logo and trademark firms to consider as well, depending on your needs and budget.

Once you've located a satisfactory designer, you should try hard to articulate the unique philosophies, concepts and output of your organization, to get him started. Expect a lively dialog with your logo designer. Since you are the founder of your business, you probably know best what you want your firm to feel like in the marketplace. The logo designer can work these intangible things into the graphic symbol, blending deeper meanings into it.

Logo designs are supposed to be simple and eye-catching. The most effective and recognizable logos use simple color patterns and readable text. It's counter-productive and unprofessional to come up with an unnecessarily flamboyant logo. So unless you can really benefit from them, avoid complex designs with diverse combinations of colors. The primary goal in a logo is to convey the nature of your company or product to the world, not poke it in the eye!

The designer will present you with design concepts to let you pick one to finalize. It should be memorable and satisfy the organization's needs. And it should be innovative and unlike any other logo in the world.

If you are working with a full-scale logo design company, there could also be a panel of specialists that goes through systematic and detailed analysis for you. If you're on our own and don't feel comfortable making final choices, either bring along someone you trust or show the designs to lots of people for their feedback. This way, the process should produce a logo that truly reflects your vision of the organization's nature.

Reliable services permit a client to request revisions or refinements of the winning concept. Once a final one is selected, the designer may need to work out the many ways it will appear: on paper, products, vehicles, in black/white only and in color, etc. A perfectly designed logo allows an innocent bystander to correctly get the feel of an organization.

Since your logo is your face in the world, having a professional design it is a prudent investment. It also goes a long way to making your new business feel real.

The Importance of Domain Names

*If no one searches for your business online, how can
they find your website?*

MOST ENTREPRENEURS believe that it their website work is done if they
purchase one or more domain names that either exactly match or capture most
of their business's name. I disagree. Of course, it is important to own the rights
to your own business's name as a URL. However, once you own it, you are safe.
Apart from making sure to renew the domain ownership contract, you won't have
to worry about someone trying to build a website that plays off of your business's
name and reputation, assuming good intentions prevail.

What many entrepreneurs don't understand is how search engines work
and what that means for domain names. Search engines determine a website's
relevancy to a query by attempting to match the keyword phrases a surfer submits
during a query (what you'd type into the topic line in Google, for example) with
the keywords that make up a website's domain name or URL.

In order to connect your business most frequently with surfers using these
search engines, think long and hard about what words your target audience will
use when searching on the web. If you are an accountant in the Chicago area and
your firm is called Tom's Bookkeeping, don't build a website using the domain
name www.TomsBookkeeping.com, even though you own it. Why? If you want
to acquire new customers via search engines, you must realize that they will never
begin by searching for Tom's Bookkeeping.

Instead, buy the domain name www.chicagolandaccounting.com (or some-
thing to that effect) and use that. Why? Because it's more likely that people in the
Chicago area will make general queries for Chicago Accounting or Chicagoland
Accounting.

Before you set out to buy every domain name that consists of keywords or
keyword phrases related to your business, product, service or industry, remember

that registrants already hold most one- and two-word domain names. The idea of purchasing large volumes of domain names for future resale has been around for over a decade. Most keyword matches or close matches related to your business are probably taken. If you feel it's crucial to your business, you can contact the owner of names you want. You may have to negotiate the price of the domain names you want, but they may be for sale.

Don't worry. If you can't get what you want, or you're wondering about whether to build a website based your business name domain or a product or industry-specific URL, remember that you can always set up what's called a permanent 301-redirect (which redirects surfers from one URL to another). That will forward individuals from one domain to another, in the event that someone types in www.yourbusinessname.com. Just make sure that the domain name that you believe will capture the most website traffic is the primary one associated with your website.

The Difference Between Copyrights and Trademarks

Ensure that you're protecting your intellectual property the right way.

BLACKSMITHS WHO MADE swords in the Roman Empire may have been the first trademark users. In later times, copyright law applied only to the copying of books. Patents are recorded as early as 500 BC among the Greeks, giving people who invented new recipes one year's exclusive use of the dish.

Protection of your intellectual property (IP) should be your very first step when starting a new business or project that depends on your IP. Also, just because you've conjured up a great concept or idea doesn't mean that you're the first to come up with it. Do yourself a favor before you start marketing your new idea and check with the appropriate government offices in order to ensure that you're not accidentally taking credit for something someone else has already registered or copyrighted.

Below is a list of Fun Facts that you may not have known about copyright and trademarking. These similar, but legally different, protection practices cover different things. By all means, seek legal advice if you have any questions on these subjects.

A copyright is a set of exclusive rights granted by a state to the creator of an original work (or the creator's assignee) for a limited period of time, upon disclosure of the work. This includes the right to copy, distribute and adapt the work.

A trademark is a distinctive sign or indicator used by an individual, business organization, or other legal entity, used to identify that the products or services to consumers with which the trademark appears originate from a unique source, and to distinguish its products or services from those of other entities.

A copyright protects works of authorship as fixed in a tangible form of expression. Examples of what a copyright covers include works of art, photos, pictures, graphic designs, drawings, songs, music and sound recordings of all kinds, books, manuscripts, publications and other written works, plays, software, movies, shows, and other performance arts. If you are interested in protecting a title, slogan, or other short word phrase, then generally, you want a trademark.

© is the copyright symbol in a copyright notice

™ is the symbol for an unregistered trademark (a mark to promote a brand or goods)

SM is the symbol for an unregistered service mark (a mark to promote or brand services)

® is the symbol for a registered trademark and a registered service mark

In the US, copyright is obtained through the United States Copyright Office (USCO), which is a division of the Library of Congress (see www.copyright.gov). Other countries have similar offices, which you can locate on the web.

Likewise, in the US, trademark is obtained through the United States Patent and Trademark Office (USPTO, at www.uspto.gov). Check the web for other countries' offices.

Keep in mind that there may be occasions when both copyright and trademark protection are desirable for the same project. For example, a marketing campaign for a new product may introduce a new slogan for use with the product, which also appears in advertisements for the product. The advertisement's text and graphics, as published, are covered by copyright. That will not, however, protect the slogan in your ad. The slogan may be protected by trademark law, but that law will not cover the rest of the advertisement. If you want both forms of protection, you will have to perform both types of registration with the appropriate offices.

The websites of the respective offices of control in countries around the world offer a wealth of further information, ranging from tutorials and step-by-step walk-throughs to other valuable information that can get you on your way to protecting your intellectual property. Don't neglect to do so.

How to Patent a New Product

A step-by-step guide to getting your product patented.

ALL TOO OFTEN, we hear about peoples' dreams of starting a business being bogged down by government paperwork. They complain that because of it, their great plans to start a new business based on a product or invention they have developed never get off the ground. The patenting process seems too overwhelming to them.

Take Europe, for example. Presently, although there exists a mechanism through the European Patent Office (EPO) for challenging and verifying a granted patent's validity, the process is limited to a nine-month period of opposition, beginning the day the patent is granted. Beyond that, a centralized way of challenging a patent granted by the EPO does not exist. Contracting states of the EPO must each separately validate a granted patent. It then becomes the responsibility of each contracting state to enforce and challenge the granted rights. It's truly a bureaucratic maze. (More information for obtaining a patent in Europe can be found at www.epo.org.)

For entrepreneurs in Australia, the patent process is very similar to that of the US. The patenting process in Australia begins at www.ipaustralia.gov.au and roughly follows the same steps as the US procedure.

Here is a step-by-step guide, with the US procedures serving as an example, to getting past the patent paperwork and on your way to building your new business.

1. First, you need to find out if your product has already been patented. You can accomplish this by running a simple search with the United States Patent and Trademark Office (USPTO) on their website, www. uspto.gov. If you discover that someone has already patented your idea, then sorry: Unless you think of a new way to use your product, there isn't much you can do.

2.   If your product hasn't already been patented, your next step is to decide what type of patent you want to apply for. There are three types: (1) Design Patents (for ornamental characteristics), (2) Plant Patents (for new varieties of asexually produced plants), or the most common (3) Utility Patents (for useful processes, machines, articles of manufacture, or the composition of matter).

3.   Once you decide which of the three types of patents fits your idea best, you must determine a filing strategy. Decide whether you want to file in the US only, or if you want International Protection. International Protection involves international cooperation among various worldwide Intellectual Property Offices. If you foresee international business, it's best to go with International Protection.

4.   Assuming that you want to file a Utility Patent, which is the most common type, you will next need to decide if you want to file a Provisional or Non-Provisional Application. Don't be scared by the long words. Basically, Provisional filings are informal and rather quick, while Non-Provisional filings are formal and involve a much more tedious process. While the Provisional process is easier, we recommend taking the time and effort, if possible, to protect your idea more fully by completing the Non-Provisional Application process.

5.   The fifth step is optional. It is expedited examination. The USPTO offers an Accelerated Examination Program whereby, basically, if you meet certain qualifications, you can "jump the line" and get your patent processed faster.

6.   Now you're ready to make the final decision before filing: Who will actually do it? Will you file yourself (which is called *pro se*) or use a registered attorney or agent? While many people undertake the process of filing themselves, we recommend that you use an attorney or agent to complete the actual filing. This will ensure that your application is not returned or delayed for inadequate completion. This is a perfect example of having to spend a little money to make money, but it's definitely worth it in the long run.

7.   Next, you or your attorney or agent gather needed elements for electronic filing. Here, you determine your application processing fees and apply for a customer number and digital certificate. You can do all this directly on the USPTO website. Your customer number allows you to easily manage all of your filings and correspondence with the USPTO and your digital certificate is a security measure that will uniquely iden-

tify you and allow you secure access to your patent information and data.

8.   Now it's time to actually apply for your patent. In the US, we recommend that you use the USPTO's Electronic Filing System (EFS) as a registered eFiler. Using the EFS, anyone with an Internet connection can file patent applications and documents without downloading special software or changing document preparation tools and processes.

9.   The good news about the ninth step is that you don't have to do anything! After you (or your attorney or agent) have completed the eighth step and submitted your application, the ninth step involves the USPTO's examination of your application. You can check your application status at any point on the website, using your Customer Number and Digital Certificate from Step 7. At the end of this step, if the USPTO gives you a "thumbs up" and your application is accepted, congratulations! Jump down to Step 12!

10.   If the USPTO doesn't accept your application on the first try, it's no big deal. Don't get discouraged. You have several options here. You can file replies, requests for reconsideration, and appeals as necessary.

11.   This step is another one in which you need not take any action. Step 11 is the USPTO's reply to your request or appeal from Step 10. If, after your appeal or request, the USPTO decides to overturn their rejection and accepts your application, they will send you a Notice of Allowance and charge you for any fees that you may owe from their additional attention.

12.   The good news, if you've made it to this point in the patent filing process, is that your patent has been accepted and only one small step stands in your way before your patent is granted! The bad news is that now, you have to pay the issuing and publication fees. Once the USPTO processes your payment, the patent is granted and your product is protected.

13.   One final step involves the preservation of your protection. Maintenance fees are due at 3.5, 7.5, and 11.5 years after the initial patent is granted.

It must be said that the United States Patent and Trademark Office has done an exceptional job streamlining their electronic filing and informational system. In the US, patenting through the USPTO is the only recognized option, but they make it easy and affordable. To learn more, see their website at www.uspto.gov.

"The Name's Bond—Surety Bond"

You might be licensed and insured, but are you bonded?

OCCASIONALLY, a small business, especially one performing contracting services, is asked to bond its work in advance. In some states, certain types of contractors are required to be bonded.

Simply put, a bond is a financial guarantee that you will honor a business contract. Sometimes referred to as a *surety bond*, a bond is a promise by a third party to pay if a vendor does not fulfill its valid obligations under a contract. There are various types of bonds, such as license bonds, performance bonds, bid bonds, indemnity bonds, and payment bonds.

- A *license* bond is required by some localities for certain businesses. In some cases, you pay the locality directly rather than obtaining a bond.

- A *performance* bond is a guarantee that you will perform work in accordance with the terms of a contract.

- A *bid* bond is a guarantee you will perform work if you win a bidding contest.

- An *indemnity* bond promises to reimburse losses incurred if you fail to perform or if you fail to pay other vendors in the fulfillment of a contact.

- A *payment* bond promises that you will pay all subcontractors and material providers utilized in the performance of a contract.

It is important to remember that a bond is *not* an insurance policy. A bond only provides assurance that the contracted work will be satisfactorily completed. For example, your bond will not pay for property damage or personal injury resulting from your work. For this, you need conventional insurance coverage.

A simple Google search will list companies that provide bonding services under *surety bonds* in your area. In general, bonding companies will only provide bond coverage up to an amount that you can cover with existing liquid assets.

Before you purchase a bond from any bonding company, have the bond documentation reviewed by your attorney and ensure that you understand exactly what the bond can and cannot protect against. This will benefit both you and your customer.

The Greatest Start-Up Challenges

Regardless of your industry, these are the most common challenges. Start preparing for them now.

WHILE STARTING A BUSINESS is always, well, *challenging*, there are a few common challenges that we see across the whole spectrum of start-ups, regardless of the type of business, business sector, or activity. By identifying these common challenges, you can plan for them, coasting over them rather than crashing headlong into them.

If you are like most entrepreneurs in the very early stages of starting a business, you are its only employee and thus, you do every single job. In short, it's all yours: from balancing the books to the creative design, from coming up with an initial marketing initiative to seeking sources of funding. Furthermore, until you're ready or able to pay someone else to do it, be prepared to paint your own office, stuff your own envelopes, sweep your own floor, or if you're opening a pet store, clean out your own cages! The more complex areas like bookkeeping or marketing design may not always be your strongest, so be prepared to ask for help.

When starting a new business, time is always of the essence, because time is money. Not just making it, but also spending it. Be prepared to learn a lot of new things, and learn them *quickly*. The quicker you learn, the faster your growth, and the faster your first real paycheck will arrive.

When you're starting a small business, time management is all. It is the foundation of everything. Without good time management, you can't possibly do everything yourself. You will inevitably waste time and learn everything slowly, and your cash flow will fly out the window faster than a frightened parakeet on speed. Compartmentalize your tasks and don't be a scatterbrain. Finish each task before you move on to the next one. The only appropriate deviation from this plan is if you rely on outside resources and you have to pause in the middle of something to receive someone else's contribution, whether it be a design conversion, a lawyer's signature, goods, etc., before you can continue.

As most experienced entrepreneurs come to realize, most things never go as planned. In business, you are constantly affected by outside factors—customers, consultants, the weather, the competition, the bank, etc. The bad news is that you typically can't control any of those things, so keeping your cash flow under control is a huge challenge. Before you even get your first customer, you'll have to purchase supplies, incur government paperwork fees, pay for your initial marketing and logo design, etc. Be ready for these things and don't be shocked if you have to pay quite a few bills before your first income arrives.

Finally, stay focused and maintain balance. Once you've compartmentalized…prioritize! When you're starting a business, your greatest priority is to finish the revenue-bearing projects first. Don't waste your time going out to buy coffee and pencils when you have a deadline pending. On the other hand, don't put off thinking of a name for a new product, if you can't launch it until you've got one!

At the start of each day, ask yourself, "What things can I do today that will have the greatest impact on my business's success?"

CHAPTER IV

Stayin' Alive

Getting Business in Old and New Ways

Chances are, if you are reading this book, you have thought a lot about how to get business. The new way forward begins here.

TODAY, the environment in which small businesses function is transforming with unending, real-time change. New strategies, technologies and trends are rapidly reshaping the way business is transacted, influencing the ways in which service is provided and products are marketed and sold. Your knowledge of and response to these trends is crucial to the success of your enterprise.

Often, small businesses suffer downturns without a discernible reason. The physician who is best-known and considered tops in his specialty, the construction company which has the most skilled laborers and has been in business for decades, and the interior designer with a large clientele and a shelf full of awards can still see downturns. They ask, "Where are the referrals?" or "Why are sales down this quarter?" or "Why did so few people come to my spring showing?"

These questions concern every business owner. Regardless of the size of your business, it is vital that you understand the importance of staying relevant and maintaining market share, using both old and new approaches. Traditional marketing, enhanced by your web-based presence, online marketing, advertising and social media initiatives, gives you a powerful toolbox that you can use to reach new prospects for your products or services.

Some entrepreneurs ignore the newer methods and rely solely on basic tried-and-true, traditional marketing approaches. Doing so limits your chances of success in today's ultra-competitive market. The important question is which approaches will benefit *your* new business. The answer is probably a combination of both old and new methods.

Sometimes, in order to regain a competitive edge, or for the sheer sake of survival, wholesale changes in your marketing approach is required. However, for most businesses, the solution is quite simple: Stay on course but improve upon the current practice, using some fresh perspectives and new or additional marketing approaches.

Deciding how to go forward always requires knowledge of the past. Historically, sales, customer service, and the bottom line have been the key focus of businesses in maintaining profitability and market share. While these elements remain critical to success, business today is much more intricate and fluid. New buyers, especially younger, more tech-savvy individuals, increasingly use online access and digital formats to learn about and buy the products and services they seek. And that goes for what they buy as consumers, as well as for their purchasing decisions at work.

Let's take a look at a simple example. Marylou loves making clay pots and other ceramics. She wants to turn her hobby into a business and sell them. Traditional marketing would point her to a hand-painted sign on the road beside her workshop, holiday flyers stuffed in neighbors' mailboxes, renting a table at potters' shows or flea markets, and so forth. And she no doubt will get some business via those approaches. But she can also easily buy a URL, construct her own website featuring photos of her pots taken with her digital camera, buy some keywords on Google, and work her Facebook and other social media networks to launch her little business. It would be a mistake for her to think that just because hers will be a very small business, she can't do all that. And she can still sell at those potters' shows!

So the new way forward for virtually all businesses requires combining traditional with new ways to market. For aspiring entrepreneurs, new businesses, and even for established businesses, embracing new and innovative avenues of marketing, advertising, networking and consumer outreach is absolutely crucial. Simply put, for growth, complacency is never the solution.

Imagine the doctor presenting an online medical seminar to the public, or the decorator showcasing her latest work with high resolution photos and videos on several social media sites. Each initiative reaches new audiences never touched before through traditional methods.

Establishing a new way forward for your business starts with research and discussions regarding which method(s) and project(s) are best for your needs. Often, this process can change the manner in which you actually do business with your clients. It's true: Learning a new way to market may take some effort. But the payoff—doing it right and reaching buyers you never would have touched—can generate new successes.

The Importance of Legal and Accounting Representation

Don't mistake these important investments for things that belong in your "unnecessary costs" pile.

IN ORDER TO CREATE a business that will thrive despite all the fluctuations in your industry, you need extraordinary planning as well as exceptional analysis. Two of the most important (and most commonly overlooked) areas are the legal and accounting resources of your business.

When you start developing your business, you will need to address your accounting and legal needs. Very small businesses that are owned by a sole proprietor or run by a partnership of a few people can realistically perform their own accounting and bookkeeping. Similarly, for legal representation, the very small business can develop a relationship with a general practice lawyer who will look into things when the need arises. However, for companies with a much larger structure, this has to be handled differently. Larger companies need to employ an accountant. Depending on how big the company is, the business may even need to enlist the help of banking professionals for some accounting needs.

Accounting representation for your business is also important as it enables you to accurately assess the financial performance of your business. Documents such as financial statements, cash flow statements, and even balance sheets give you an indication of how well your business is doing. This, in turn, enables you to plan your response if the business is making losses. Unless you are an accountant yourself, if you lack accounting representation, you may not have an accurate idea of where your business is headed. And it's always good to have an objective view on your company's financial health.

The same applies for the legal representation of a large business. Larger companies are better off retaining a corporate lawyer or law firm to handle their legal representation, as a general practice lawyer would find the workload too spe-cialized and overwhelming.

Before you sign a contract with anyone to do either your accounting or legal representation, ensure that you have done the proper background check and per-formance research. Do so no matter whether your representatives are in a small or a large firm, as the ramifications are the same if your representatives prove to be unscrupulous or incompetent. Getting the right legal and accounting representa-tion will prevent avoidable problems.

One major mistake that most businesses make when they begin to become successful is that they forget the importance of legal representation as well as ac-counting representation. Instead, they focus on customer service. And while that should not be neglected, neither should the financial and legal part of the business. Knowledgeable, accurate legal and accounting representation can make huge dif-ference in the success of a business.

One final note: Select advisors who naturally want to educate you about their specialty. You won't become a lawyer or accountant, but you'll learn to think like they do and be a better leader and planner. And you can save billable hours, when you handle the things you can safely do in house.

How to Write a Press Release

Use these proven ideas when developing effective press releases and impress your target audiences while achieving Search Engine Optimization (SEO) success.

- Our first tip is simple—use your business **logo** whenever possible and don't miss out on an opportunity to build brand recognition. Make sure that your business's logo is on all of its press releases, preferably near the top, so the viewers can't miss seeing it.

- Ensure that the press release includes real **news**. The press release also needs to draw positive attention to your business.

- Include the **main point** of the press release in the headline, subheading and in the first paragraph. Most viewers only read the first couple of paragraphs of press releases. And for search engine indexing purposes, remember that the most relevant content should be in the beginning of the press release.

- Create a concise **headline**, typically not more than twenty words, that covers the key message of the press release. Remember that search engines and other types of software and crawler programs can't usually "get" any hidden meanings, puns or marketing slogans. Therefore clean and understandable headlines perform best for maximizing the popularity and ranking of your press release. At the same time, remember that some people *are* more inclined to read further into clever headlines. This isn't a Catch-22, but be sure to use reason and logic when creating a headline to attract and hold the potential viewing audience.

- Use **subheads** (sub-headlines) strategically. Subheads offer you the ability to provide additional information to viewers when they are deciding if they want to continue reading the press release. To enhance your Search

Engine Optimization (SEO), a subhead is a wonderful spot to work in keywords and keyword phrases that had to be left out of the primary headline.

- Provide **links** in the beginning of the press release and continue to include them frequently. Appropriate links, in the form of anchor-text and hyperlinks, assist search engines as they index the press release by associating the content of the press release with other related content sources and sites. This strategy provides additional context to readers of the press release. Always link the first mention of a brand or product name that is being discussed to the appropriate landing page on your business's website. Also, be sure to create links for the names in a press release to individual biographies or their social media profile page(s).

- You wouldn't think this needs to be mentioned, but be sure to provide accurate, complete **contact information**. Don't discover you forgot to include it or you never changed the information after the company changed addresses, phone numbers, or points of contact. Seriously, it happens. Ensure that your readers have the necessary information to contact your business. This includes the name and title of the contact, address, phone number(s), fax number, emails, social media links, website, and any other means of communication that you have available for individuals or businesses to reach you.

- Don't forget to **format**. Not unlike other media outlets, the presentation of the information is crucial. Be sure to use things like underlining, bullets, and bold or italic fonts to help convey all important parts of the press release. If the press release uses standard font and permits limited formatting, separate content so the reader can move through the press release in manageable pieces. Remember college textbooks? Same concept. Make key words and phrases stand out so that busy readers can still understand the message, even with limited reading time.

- In the event that your business is publicly traded, provide the specific exchange, the **company's ticker or stock symbol**, and its International Securities Identifier Number. By including these pieces of information, the press release will become easier to find in a multitude of news networks and databases.

- Use **multimedia**. Whether it is a random reader, an avid consumer or journalist, most people prefer to look at something with supporting media, such as pictures, videos or audio clips. Studies have shown that press releases with multimedia content are more likely to be viewed.

Small Business Tax Tips

Taxes can be a cinch if addressed right, or a nightmare if addressed wrong. Here are some tips to keep your business ready for your tax due date at all times.

TO MANAGE A NEW BUSINESS WELL, you need to know how to effectively file the business's taxes. All business owners are expected to file tax data once a year. It doesn't matter whether you are making a profit or reporting losses. While most people find this process quite daunting, it doesn't have to be that way. All you really need to ensure is that you have the appropriate tools to aid you in the process, as well as the appropriate people. The following tips should make filing taxes a bit easier for any small business owner.

The first thing you need to do is to ensure that someone with impeccable bookkeeping skills is keeping track of things for your business. Now is not the time to be overzealous; if you can't do it properly yourself, hire someone who can. Most business owners find bookkeeping quite intimidating. If you can't do it thoroughly professionally yourself, we strongly suggest that you hire a professional to do it for you.

If you're on the fence, keep in mind that outsourcing this task isn't nearly as daunting as being audited by your country's tax regulatory authority. Although you pay an accredited accountant or bookkeeper, at least you can be sure that you are not making losses due to poor accounting. If your bookkeeping is shoddy, it will be reflected in the financial statements. This will make it even more difficult to file the business's taxes.

Like attorneys or real estate agents, bookkeepers do not have to be hired as a permanent employees. Small businesses can hire good bookkeepers once a month for several hours or a couple of days, depending on how much work needs to be done. Most short-term bookkeepers charge on an hourly basis. After they are done putting the books in order, you can choose to either let them file your tax returns for you, or you can do this on your own. If you let them do it for you, they will have to keep the records so that they can take them to your country's tax regulatory authority on your behalf.

Another thing you can do to keep your tax filing hassle-free is to have all the documents pertaining to your business in order before you file. Filing taxes for small businesses requires you to be meticulous. If any of the miscellaneous documents are missing, the process can be dragged out for months. So establish a filing system from the very start of your business so that you can have all the necessary paperwork in order. Just because it is a filing system for a business doesn't mean that it has to be complicated. Make it as simple and as logical as you can so that you can easily track whatever paperwork you may need for the process. A good tip: Get advice from your bookkeeper or accountant on how to set up your files and on what to keep (and what not) to document your taxable activities.

Another convenient way to ensure that your tax filing is hassle-free is to file your taxes with the use of online software. The great thing about this is that your business's tax information will be stored on the server for several years, so you can always double-check it whenever you want.

Hiring: Talent, Loyalty and Age

Employees jumping ship may cause your business to sink. Consider both talent and the potential for loyalty when you hire.

NOWADAYS, BUSINESSES, especially small business, and *especially* new, small businesses, are just trying to stay afloat. They are trying to establish themselves and keep their doors open by supplying their customers with the best products and services available. They rely on superior talent as a strategic advantage.

Why? More often than not, a superior team produces a superior product. The team with the most talent, the most (or best) education, and the most experience will deliver the best product. The issue that most entrepreneurs face, however, is how to get the best products or services out of the best team members they can afford to employ.

You may not have a big budget for salaries and benefits, so you may turn to relatively young workers whose income expectations match your budget best. You'll not be buying experience, but you may get extra energy, newer schooling and thinking, and an ability to share your vision that more seasoned workers may lack.

But you'll have to consider another issue: loyalty. Business owners have found that a company filled with new people (regardless of talent or age) will not perform as well as a team that has worked together on multiple projects for an extended period of time. During an employment interview, the applicant's potential loyalty can often count more than her credentials.

Consider this: Most businesses' daily tasks lie beyond the scope of typical education. What an applicant learned in school might not have anything to do with what your company is currently working on. This fact, plus the fact that it costs your company a lot of time and money to train someone and get her up to speed, means that you don't want to hire someone who is unsure about how long she plans to stay with your company.

It may be wiser to try for a mix of older and younger talent, as best you can afford it, with the strategy of encouraging everybody to share their strongest suits with the rest of the team. Your older employees may feel loyal because they are less sure of their job mobility, and your younger ones may feel like staying for the fun and challenge of this new business.

As an entrepreneur you want to hire smart, and also create a workplace based on mutual trust, where each of your employees wants to stay and grow. You'll certainly want to ask about candidates' dream jobs and where they want to be in five years. But the more you can build trust and engage their dreams with yours, the longer your team will gain loyalty, knit together and produce the results you all want.

CHAPTER V
When Tomorrow Becomes Today

Starting a Web-Based Business

Don't make the mistake of thinking that your web-based business shouldn't be run like a storefront business. Without proper planning, you'll fail just as fast.

THERE ARE MANY STEPS to starting a web-based business or even adding an electronic component to your brick-and-mortar business—everything from building an e-commerce website, setting up merchant banking, and creating marketing, to developing the necessary wholesale distribution relationships. The first of the necessary steps is, naturally, to develop the idea. Then you create your general business plan, deciding what your business will look like, and defining how and why your model will work, compared to the competition.

During the development stage of the web-based business planning process, it is important to flesh out all your ideas pertaining to the venture. Identify prospects, where to sell, how to market, and what to expect in expense and revenue numbers. Remember to write up a business plan just as you would any other business. Don't forget to factor in all logical contingencies. If you intend to acquire outside financing, make sure to stay on top of listing expenses exclusive to your web-based business like web-hosting fees, graphic design, and any other technology costs for hardware or software.

After your business plan is laid out and plans have been put into place, it is time to build the necessary distribution relationships. The most common approach is to seek out a nationwide wholesaler and inquire about account possibilities. Often, this level of distributorship charges a small fee and yields emerging businesses with very competitive bottom lines.

After that segment of development, it is a good idea to get started on your e-commerce website. The website should be very easy to navigate and provide visitors with the most up-to-date information regarding your company and the products or services you offer. Don't be fooled! Constructing a good site takes time and patience. Many websites offer only a small variety of products and have minimal information. It is important to spend the necessary time developing your site, always keeping your prospective buyers in mind, especially if the web is going to be your primary medium of exposure.

The website should provide everything a prospect may want to know: an extensive database of your products or services, including clearly readable titles, pictures, detailed descriptions and prices, if possible; also contact and "about us" information. Make sure to list your business on eBay, Amazon and other e-commerce compilers. Also, create different forms of search queries that make referencing your product catalog easy.

Next, during the merchant phase, choose a service provider that has a great track record. You don't want to get caught in a situation where transactions are not going through for reasons unknown to you or due to poor customer service. Look for reasonable monthly fees and nominal transaction costs that you feel are congruent with your business model. The easiest way to accomplish this is to study your competition. Make sure you can accept e-checks and PayPal; happily, these two forms of payment are very common in the online world.

When setting up your online merchant banking, remember two important things: first, make sure you have security in place to temporarily hold unusual transactions, such as those coming from IP addresses foreign to the billing address or ones with limited customer information. Second, allow yourself the ability to authorize virtual transactions via your personal computer or application. This makes doing business on the go or over the phone extremely convenient.

From there, develop your marketing. Build e-mailers that you can send to pre-paid list recipients or existing customers. Make sure there is plenty of fulfillment material. Most consumers respond to collateral sales material more than anything because it is coming from a trusted source. Think about industry events, blogs, chat rooms, and magazines.

Just as for a business with a tangible brick-and-mortar store-front, planning and research are key in the success of a web-based business.

Making Sure People Find Your Internet Business

Small, subtle website tweaks and adjustments can skyrocket popularity. Here's why.

DO YOU EVER wonder why websites change? Maybe it's the colors, the navigation icons, or content changes. Most changes that occur on websites are not random. They are typically very specific changes that the Webmaster or site owner has decided to make because of analytics and test results from a multitude of fronts.*

Think of your website as a racecar. Even if it looks great and sounds great, there is still some fine-tuning that can be done to achieve peak performance. With a little tweak here and a small adjustment there, a handful of minute adjustments can easily produce noticeable results. Most adjustments are as easy as choosing one word over another. Ensure that you change little things, frequently—every day, if possible. For the powers that that be who make your website popular, changing one word every day for 100 days is much better than changing 100 words in one day. While it's not quite that simple, that's the basic idea.

In a web-based business, many different components exist beyond most individuals' field of vision. Quite often, business owners or website creators attempt to conceptualize what they think is a perfect website without focusing on things like analytics, Internet marketing, social media, and search engine optimization (SEO). If these critical items are not addressed, a website, no matter how well-built, will struggle to survive in a sea of websites and web pages that *are* making the necessary efforts to generate site traffic and get exposure across multiple platforms. Below are a few tools commonly used. And good news: They are usually available free.

---

*In the interest of keeping this section quick to read, we have not defined a number of technical terms. You can find the definitions in the Glossary.

An easy first step is implementing a very **basic analytics program**. This code can easily be placed on every site page throughout your entire website. Analytics are a must, due to the immeasurable value they offers site owners, developers or Webmasters. With analytics properly installed on every page, then validated, business owners can track visitors in multiple capacities, reporting the number of page views, how long viewers stayed on the website, bounce rates, and other relevant metrics that are vital to the survival of a newly emerging website.

Another simple tactic used to maximize the effectiveness of a website is to set up a **Webmaster program** to better track the metrics associated with your website. These are a must. Be sure to look at things like crawl reports, indexed pages, and indexation issues; and also track basic statistics such as clicks, keywords and other traffic metrics. It is important to continually improve your website, to be sure that it is being ranked properly. Don't be afraid to make adjustments to enhance viewer retention.

After you have installed an analytics program and a Webmaster tool, it would be wise to run a **crawl simulation**. The purpose of a crawl simulation is to shed light on anything that was overlooked during the final phases of website development. Running a crawl simulation will bring most unknown errors, incomplete redirects, broken links, and missing titles to your attention, allowing you to make immediate repairs. Every day that a site is live is potentially a day on which it could be re-crawled by spiders. If this happens, you want to make sure that you have made the necessary changes to fix any existing mistakes, especially items mentioned above like improper redirects, broken links, files blocked by robot.txt and missing tags. These crawl simulations can be administered by *free* programs found on the web, or they can be purchased. Either way you go, it is crucial to run a crawl simulation.

Once the crawl simulation is complete, it is time to test your website, or more specifically, its design, with a **browser emulator**. Browser emulators are used to confirm that the design, layout and imagery work well and look great on multiple browsing platforms such as Safari, Internet Explorer, Firefox, Google Chrome, and anything else that you would like to check. This is also a great time to address any framing issues with mobile devices. In our era of mobile devices, such as smart phones and tablets, be sure that if you intend to be viewed on these devices, your website is formatted properly to automatically frame to their screen sizes.

If your website is going to offer an **RSS Feed** (which it should), then you need to outfit it with analytics to track the performance of the feed. There isn't too much mystery here. It is important to understand the metrics associated with your feed and making changes accordingly.

At some point, you will need to compile a **list of contacts**. This list should include everyone, ranging from colleagues, business contacts, and friends to family.

These individuals can be instrumental in building that much-needed buzz when you launch a fresh, new website. Also, it would be wise to send out a few emails inviting your contacts to check out the site and give honest feedback. The communication can be created as a formal press release, a snail mail letter, or even a casual email with a strongly personal feel. We recommend some kind of middle ground. Make sure it's not a pitching or selling message, but do be sure to add a touch of pride and professionalism to your communication.

Essentially, there are many ways to properly plan, prepare and monitor a website during every stage of its development. These few steps are extremely easy to implement and they can help not only Webmasters, but website and business owners, in their quest to enhance and improve the quality of their website and its performance. Good luck! We hope you find these tools useful in the continued evolution of your web-based business.

Afterword:
Where to Go from Here?

IT MAY BE SAFE TO ASSUME that if you've just finished reading this book, you are one of two types of individuals. The *curious* reader may have been interested in learning how a potentially successful business could be envisioned, created and then finally launched to compete in the marketplace. For curious readers, these pages may have even sparked your imagination about becoming an entrepreneur one day. Curious readers have always shown interest in educating and informing themselves on a new topic and enhancing their knowledgebase while doing so.

The *serious* reader may have chosen to read our book because he or she may have already decided to toss a hat in the ring and become an entrepreneur. Or perhaps, you've launched your business, and now additional tools, expert guidance, and real-world examples are vital to your success. A serious reader never stops perusing every possible source for innovative ideas, the next greatest trend, or even a leg up on the competition.

Curious or serious, we hope that everyone who has read this first volume of our series found the material worthy of your time. Regardless of how or why you found us, we are glad you did.

For the guys who wrote this first volume, and also founded the Expert Business Advice website, the philosophy was simple:

- Create material of substance and value that can continue to be expanded indefinitely for the benefit of the reader, the customer, and the business professional
- Deliver the best possible ideas, resources and guidance to those who seek it
- Take ownership of our work, stand by it, and be proud of it

Developing this material from several points of view and delivering it to people from diverse backgrounds and with multiple levels of experience was crucial for us. In fact, it was the only way we could imagine doing it.

Simply put, our goal with this series shares the same vision as our own company's slogan: "Experts Create | We Deliver | You Apply."

The way forward begins here…

Acknowledgements

WE HAVE A LOT OF THANKS TO GIVE.

Scott wishes to thank his wife Kellin, his co-authors, his parents, the Girard Family, the Conway Family, the Edwards Family, the Seaman Family, the Warren Family (keep up the writing, Lea), the O'Keefe Family, everyone at Pinpoint Holdings Group, Barbara Stephens, Jack Chambless, Mary-Jo Tracy, Sandra McMonagle, Diane Orsini, Nathan Holic, Peter Telep, Pat Rushin, the Seminole Battalion, Dawn Price, and the Republic of Colombia (for the sweet, sweet brown nectar which fueled this project).

Mike wishes to thank his parents Tim and Gaye O'Keefe, his co-authors, Jamie, Kimberly Rupert, the O'Keefe Family, the Goldsberry Family, the Roy Family, the Hubert Family, the Murat Family, the Grant Family, the Girard Family, the Price Family, the Holycross Family, the most inspiring professor Jack Chambless, his two favorite authors Clive Cussler and Timothy Ferriss, and those individuals in Argentina (for making sure there is always Malbec on the table).

Marc wishes to thank his wife Dawn, his co-authors, his mom Lynda, the Price Family, the O'Bryan Family, the Smith Family, Jean Hughes, Kellin Girard, Mike Schiano, and his life-long mentor Howard Satin.

The authors would collectively like to thank Kathe Grooms and everyone at Nova Vista Publishing, everyone at Expert Business Advice, Jon Collier, and the Van Beekum Family: Dave, Melissa and the Sugar Gliders.

Glossary

301-redirect	A method of communicating to web browsers and search engines that a web page or site has been permanently moved to a new location. A 301-redirect should be used whenever a website is moved to a new domain name (URL).
Accountant	One who is trained and qualified in the practice of accounting or who is in charge of public or private accounts.
Accounting	The systematic recording, reporting and analysis of the financial transactions of a business or government.
Accredited Investor	A term defined by various countries' securities laws that characterizes investors permitted to invest in certain types of higher risk investments including seed money, limited partnerships, hedge funds, private placements, and angel investor networks. The term generally includes wealthy individuals and financially-oriented organizations such as banks, insurance companies, significant charities, some corporations, endowments, and retirement plans.
Acquisitions	Acquiring control of a business, called a target, by stock purchase or exchange, either hostile or friendly. Also called a takeover.
Acumen	Keenness and swiftness in understanding and dealing with a business situation in a manner that is likely to lead to a good outcome.

Advertising

A form of communication used to encourage or motivate an audience to take or continue to take some new action. Most commonly, the desired result is to guide consumer behavior regarding a commercial offering.

Analytics

The application of computer technology, operational research, and statistics to alleviate problems in business and industry.

Anchor Text

The text that composes a link to another website or resource. In the HTML link example that follows, <a href="http://www.example.com">Expert Business Advice</a>, the words "Expert Business Advice" are the anchor text.

Angel Investor

An individual who provides funding to one or more start-up companies. The individual is usually affluent or has a personal interest in the success of the venture. Such investments are distinguished by high levels of risk and a potentially large return on investment.

Balance Sheet

A quantitative synopsis of a company's financial condition at a specific point in time, including assets, liabilities and net worth. The first part of a balance sheet illustrates all the productive assets a company owns, and the second part shows all the financing methods (such as liabilities and shareholders' equity). Also called a statement of condition.

Ball-Park Figure

A figure given as an estimated value based on information available. Also called a ball park estimate.

Bid Bond

A bond purchased by a business or individual when bidding on a large project or sale, in order to demonstrate that sufficient funding exists to complete the transaction if the bidder is selected. The bond guarantees that the bidder will not be prevented from fulfilling the contract by availability by lack of funding.

Blog	A personal journal published on the Internet consisting of discrete entries, called *posts*, typically displayed in reverse chronological order so the most recent post appears first.
Blue Chip	Generally, anything of very high quality, as in blue-chip stocks.
Board of Directors	Individuals elected by a business's shareholders to oversee the management of the business.
Bonding Company	A financial entity, most commonly an insurance company, which assumes the risk of a surety bond obligee by guaranteeing payment on the bond in the event of a default or a failure of the obligee to perform its contracted services.
Bookkeeping	The systematic transcription of a business's financial transactions.
Bottom Line	The amount left after taxes, interest, depreciation, and other expenses are subtracted from gross sales. Also called net earnings, net income, or net profit.
Bounce Rate	The percentage of visitors who enter a website and immediately leave the site ("bounce") rather than continue viewing other pages within the same site.
Brainstorming	A group creativity technique in which members spontaneously and freely generate a list of ideas to address a specific opportunity or problem.
Brain-Trust Equity	Equity that is accepted or earned through an individual's contribution of information, ideas, or concepts to the strategic growth, development or direction of a company and its products, services or organizational structure.
Brand	An identifying symbol, word, phrase or mark that identifies and distinguishes a product or business from its competitors.
Branding	The act of identifying a product or business and distinguishing it from its competitors by utilizing unique symbols, words, or marks.

Brick-and-Mortar Business

A description of a company or portion of a company with a physical presence, as opposed to one that exists only virtually, on the Internet.

Broken Links

Links (either on individual websites or the Internet in general) that point to web pages, servers or other resources that have become permanently unavailable. The term also describes the effects of failing to update out-of-date web pages that clutter search engine results. Also called a dead link or dangling link.

Browser Emulator

A system that imitates the function of multiple browsers, through modifications to hardware or software, that allows the imitating system to accept the same data, execute the same programs, and achieve the same results as the imitated browser. Useful for ensuring that a website appears correctly on all types of web browsers: Mac OS, Internet Explorer, Firefox, etc.

Budget

An itemized prediction of an individual's or business's income and expenses expected for some period in the future.

Budget Deficit

The amount by which a business or individual's spending exceeds its income over a specific period of time.

Business

A commercial activity engaged in as a means of occupation or income, or an entity which engages in such activities.

Business Consultant

An individual or company that provides advising, analyzing, monitoring, training, reviewing or reporting services to commercial clients.

Business License

Permits issued by government agencies that grant individuals or companies the right to conduct business within the government's geographical jurisdiction. It is the authorization to start a new business issued by the local government.

Business Model	A description of the operations of a business including the segments of the business; its functions, roles and relationships; and the revenues and expenses that the business generates.
Business Operations	Ongoing recurring activities involved in running a business in order to generate value for its stakeholders.
Business Plan	A document prepared by a company's management, or by a consultant on their behalf, that details the past, present, and future of the company, usually for the purpose of attracting capital investment.
Business Taxes	Taxes owed and paid by a corporate entity.
Buyout	The purchase or acquisition of controlling interest in one corporation by another corporation, in order to take over assets and/or operations.
C-Corporation	A business which, unlike a partnership, is a completely separate entity from its owners. Also called a C-Corp.
Capital	1. Cash or goods used to produce income either by investing in a business or a different income property.
	2. The net worth of a company; that is, the amount by which its assets exceed its liabilities.
	3. The money, property, and other valuables which collectively represent the value of an individual or business.
Capital Expenditure	Money spent to acquire or enhance physical assets such as buildings and machinery. Also called capital spending or capital expense.
Capital Requirements	The amount of cash a business needs for its normal operations.
Cash Capital Disbursement	The repaying of a debt or expense.
Cash Flow Positive	The situation when income exceeds liabilities.
Cash Flow Statement	A summary of a business's cash flow over a given period of time.

Chat Room	Any form of online communication in which participants type and send their thoughts, taking turns sequentially, as in chatting, either in real time or asynchronously. Useful for electronic instant communication among several people.
Class A Office Space	These buildings represent the highest quality buildings available. They are generally the most attractive buildings with the best construction, and possess high quality building infrastructure. Class A buildings also are well-located, have good access, and are managed by professionals.
Class B Office Space	One notch down from Class A quality, Class B buildings are generally a little older, but are still well-managed. Often, value-added investors target these buildings as investments, since well-located Class B buildings can be returned to their Class A status through renovation such as façade and common area improvements.
Collateral	Assets pledged by a borrower to secure a loan or other credit, and subject to seizure in the event of default. Also called security.
Company Description	The third section of a business plan. A brief synopsis that describes how all of the different components in a business work together.
Competitor	A business or person that provides similar products or services.
Contingency Plan	A plan devised for an outcome other than the one in the expected plan.
Contract	A binding agreement between two or more parties for taking action, or refraining from taking action, sometimes in exchange for lawful monetary or other consideration.
Controlling Interest	The ownership of a majority of a company's voting stock; or a significant fraction, even if less than the majority, if the rest of the shares are not actively voted.

Convertible Debt	Security which can be converted for a specified amount of another, related security, at the option of the issuer and/or the holder. Also called convertible.
Copyright	The exclusive right to produce and dispose of copies of a literary, musical, or artistic work.
Corp.	The abbreviation for *corporation*.
Corporation	The most common form of business organization, which is given many legal rights as an entity separate from its owners. This form of business is characterized by the limited liability of its owners, the issuance of shares of easily transferable stock, and existence as a going concern.
Credentials	A tangible representation of qualification, competence, or authority issued to an individual by a third party with a relevant authority or assumed competence to do so.
Credit	The borrowing ability of an individual or company.
Credit History	A record of an individual's or company's past borrowing and repaying behavior.
Credit Report	A report comprised of detailed information on a person's credit history.
Credit Score	A numerically represented measure of credit risk calculated from a credit report using a standardized formula.
Creditworthiness	A creditor's measure of an individual's or company's ability to meet debt responsibilities.
Curriculum Vitae	A résumé; an overview of a person's experience and other qualifications. Also called a CV.
Customer Service	The supply of service to customers before, during and after a purchase.
Database	An organized accumulation of data, today typically in digital form. The data are typically organized to depict relevant aspects of reality, in a way that supports processes requiring this information.

Deadline   The date by which something has to be accomplished.

Debt   An amount owed to a person or organization for funds borrowed.

Debt Financing   Financing by selling bonds, bills or notes to individuals or businesses.

Debt Retirement   The repayment of a debt.

Debt-to-Income Ratio   A figure that calculates how much income is spent repaying debts.

Deduction   An expense subtracted from adjusted gross income when calculating taxable income. Also called tax deduction.

Delta   Balance. For example, when demand equals supply. Also called equilibrium. Can also mean degree of change, or change itself.

Demographics   Data on socioeconomic groups, e.g., age, income, sex, education, occupation, etc., often used to study or profile a target market.

Design Patent   A patent issued on the ornamental design of a functional item.

Disclaimer   A statement made to remove oneself from responsibility. Also called hedge clause.

Dividend   A taxable cash award declared by a company's board of directors and given to its shareholders out of the company's current or retained earnings, usually quarterly. Also used as a slang term to mean reward.

Domain Name   An identification string (sequence of letters and perhaps numbers) that defines a realm of administrative autonomy, authority, or control on the world wide web. For example, www.expertbusinessadvice.com.

Double Taxation   Taxation of the same income at two levels. One common example is taxation of earnings at the personal income level and then again at the sales level.

e-Commerce	The buying and selling of products and services by businesses and consumers through an electronic medium, without using any paper documents.
Economics	The study of how the forces of supply and demand assign scarce resources.
Economy	Activities related to the production and distribution of goods and services in a specific geographic region.
EFS	Acronym for Electronic Filing System.
Electronic Filing System	An Internet-based system for managing and organizing documents electronically.
Entrepreneur	An individual who starts his or her own business.
EPO	Acronym for European Patent Office.
Equity	Ownership interest in a business in the form of common stock or preferred stock.
Equity Financing	Financing a business by selling common or preferred stock to investors.
Establishments	Organizations.
European Patent Office	One of the two offices of the European Patent Organization. The other is the Administrative Council.
Executive Summary	The first section of a business plan. A synopsis of the entire plan, along with a brief history of the company.
Expense	Any cost of conducting business.
Expense Report	A document that contains all the expenses that a business has incurred as a result of the business's operation.
Fair Isaac Corporation	A publicly traded company that provides analytics and decision making services, including credit scoring, intended to help financial services companies make complex, high-volume decisions.
Farming Out	A slang term for outsourcing, in which organizations hire vendors to perform duties the organizations choose not to do themselves in-house.

FICO   Acronym for Fair Isaac Corporation.

Financial Adviser   A person or organization employed by a business or mutual fund to manage assets or provide investment advice.

Financials   Documents related to finance.

Financing   Providing the necessary monetary capital.

Fixed Expense   An expense that does not change depending on production or sales levels, such as rent, property tax, insurance, or interest expense. Also called fixed cost.

Forfeiture   The act of forfeiting.

Franchise   A form of business organization in which a company which already has a successful product or service (the franchisor) enters into a continuing contractual agreement with other businesses (franchisees) operating under the franchisor's trade name, usually with the franchisor's guidance, in exchange for a fee.

Franchising   The practice of licensing a successful business model.

Fulfillment   Accomplishment. Also can mean storing, order processing and shipment of goods.

Funding Request   A request for funding.

General Partner   A partner with unlimited legal obligation for the debts and liabilities of a partnership.

Grant   Funds disbursed by the grantor to a recipient.

Graphic Design   A method of artistic marketing used to create and combine words, symbols, and images to create a visual representation of ideas and messages.

Gross Margin   A measure of profitability, often shortened to GM. To calculate divide Gross Income by Net Sales, and express it as a percentage. For example, a widget sells for $5 and costs $3 to make.

                                  $5 (Net Sales) - $3 (Cost of Goods) = $2 (Gross Income).

                                  Then $2 \div 5 = 0.4$, which expressed as a percentage is 40% Gross Margin.

Growth Rate	A measure of financial growth.
Growth Strategy	A plan of action based on investing in companies and sectors which are growing faster than their peers. Also can mean an organization's plan for increasing, expanding, and otherwise getting bigger.
Hardware	A general term for equipment that can be touched. In business, *hardware* most commonly refers to computer hardware; laptops, desktops, monitors, etc. In general, computer software operates on computer hardware.
Home-Based Business	A small business that operates from the business owner's home. Also called a home business.
Hyperlink	A reference to data that the operator can directly follow, or that is followed automatically. A hyperlink points to an entire document or to a specific element within a document.
Inc.	Abbreviation for incorporated.
Income	Revenues minus cost of sales, operating expenses, and taxes, over a given period of time.
Income Statement	A document illustrating sales, expenses, and net profit for a given period.
Incorporated	A business that has been formed into a legal corporation by completing the required procedures.
Indemnity Bond	An insurance bond used as an additional measure of security to cover loan amounts, worth about 75 percent of the value of the property. This bond protects lenders from loss, in the event that the borrower defaults on the loan.
Industry Standard	A practice accepted as convention by industry members, either through formal agreement or through emulation of best practices established by industry leaders.
Initial Public Offering	The initial sale of stock by a company to the public.
Intellectual Property	Any intangible asset that is comprised of human knowledge and ideas.

Interest	The return earned on an investment.
Internal Revenue Service	The federal agency of the United States responsible for administering and enforcing the U.S. Treasury Department's revenue laws, through the assessment and collection of taxes, determination of pension plan qualification, and related activities.
International Securities Identifier Number	A exclusive international code which identifies a securities issue.
Internet	Commonly called a network of networks, the Internet is a global system of interconnected computer networks that use the standard Internet protocol suite to serve billions of users worldwide.
Internet Marketing	The marketing of products or services over the Internet. Also called web marketing, online marketing, webvertising, and e-marketing.
Internship	On-the-job training for college (or sometimes high school) students.
Interview	A discussion between two people where questions are asked by the interviewer in order to gather information from the interviewee. Often part of a hiring process.
Investment Banker	An individual who acts as an underwriter or agent for businesses and municipalities issuing securities.
Investment Group	A group of investors who pool some of their money and make joint investments. Also called an investment club.
Investor	An individual who commits monetary capital to investment products with the expectation of financial return.
IP Address	Internet Protocol Address. A numerical identification assigned to each device participating in a computer network that uses the Internet Protocol for communication.
IPO	Acronym for Initial Public Offering.
IRS	Acronym for Internal Revenue Service.

ISIN	Acronym for International Securities Identifier Number.
Keyword	A word or identifier that has a specific meaning to the programming language.
Leader	An individual who guides.
Legal Representation	An attorney. Also called a lawyer.
Lending Portfolio	A collection of investments all owned by the same person or organization.
Letter of Reference	A letter in which an employer, past or present, recommends someone for a new job. Also called a letter of recommendation.
Leveraged Buyout	The takeover of a company or controlling interest of a company (a buyout), involving a significant amount of borrowed (leveraged) money.
Liability	An obligation that legally commits an individual or company to settle a debt.
Licensing	Under defined conditions, the granting of permission to use intellectual property rights, such as trademarks, patents, or technology.
Limited Liability Company	A type of company, authorized only in certain business sectors, whose owners and managers receive the limited liability and tax benefits of an S-Corporation without having to conform to S-Corporation restrictions.
Limited Partner	In a corporate entity with one or more general partners, limited partners are liable only to the extent of their investments. Limited partners also enjoy rights to the partnership's cash flow, but are not liable for company obligations.
Links	See *hyperlinks*.
Liquidation	The process of converting assets or investments into cash.
Liquidity	The ability of an asset or property to be converted into cash quickly and without any price discount.

LLC	Acronym for limited liability company.
Loan	An arrangement in which a lender gives monetary capital or property to a borrower, and the borrower agrees to return the property or repay the monetary capital, usually along with interest, at some future point in time.
Logo	A graphic mark or wordmark used by individuals or organizations to aid and promote instant public recognition.
Mandate	A command or order.
Market Analysis	Research intended to predict the expectations of a market.
Marketing	The process by which products and services are announced and launched into the marketplace.
Marketing Plan	A written document that illustrates the necessary actions to achieve one or more marketing objectives. It can be for a product or service, a brand, or a product line.
Marketplace	The area—actual, virtual or metaphorical—in which a market operates.
Market Penetration	Occurs when a business penetrates a market in which products or services already exist.
Market Segment	A collection of consumers that share multiple characteristics(e.g., demographics, behavior, psychographic similarities, geographic relationships with unmet or underserved needs) that is large and accessible enough to present a reasonable marketing opportunity for a business.
Market Share	The percentage of the total sales of a given type of product or service that is won by given company.
Market Test	A geographic region or demographic group used to gauge the applicability of a product or service in a marketplace, prior to a wide-scale launch.
Media	Entities used to store and deliver information or data.

Merchant Banking	An investment bank which is well-equipped to manage multinational corporations. Commonly, electronic.
Middleman	Intermediary between two commercial entities, commonly a wholesaler or distributor who buys from a manufacturer and sells to a retailer or to consumer.
Mission Statement	A mission statement is a statement of the purpose of a business or organization.
Multimedia	Combined use of multiple media.
Municipality	An administrative division that has corporate status and usually self-governing powers.
NDA	Acronym for non-disclosure agreement.
Network	An arrangement of connections.
Non-Disclosure Agreement	A contract that prohibits the disclosure of confidential information or proprietary knowledge under specific circumstances.
Open Market	A market which is widely and generally accessible to all investors or consumers.
Operating Expense	An expense arising in the normal course of running a business, such as manufacturing, advertising and sales.
OPEX	Acronym for operating expense.
Outsourcing	Work executed for a business by people other than the business's full-time employees.
Over-Saturated Market	In a market occupied by buyers and sellers, a market that is filled with sellers to the point that it negatively affects each seller's opportunity to make a significant profit. Also called a saturated market.
Owner-Operated	An organization that is operated in full or in majority by its owner.
Ownership Equity	The owner's share of the assets of a business.

Partners	Members of a partnership, either general or limited.
Partnership	A relationship of two or more entities, people or companies, conducting business for mutual benefit.
Passion	Intense emotion; used in business to identify positive dedication and engagement by someone with an idea, activity, role, etc.
Patent	The exclusive right, granted by the government, to use an invention or process for a given period of time, usually 14 years.
Payment Bond	A surety bond through which a contractor assures an owner that material and labor provided in the completion of a project will be fully paid for, and that no mechanics' liens will be filed against the owner.
Performance Bond	A bond issued to guarantee adequate and acceptable completion of a project by a contractor.
Permit	The legal authorization or physical item which grants someone permission to do something.
Personal Finances	One's private funds, property, possessions. The application of finance principles to the monetary decisions of a person or family.
Press Release	A written or recorded message directed at members of the news media and others of potential interest for the purpose of announcing something newsworthy. Also called a news release, media release, or press statement.
Price Point	A point on a range of possible prices at which something might be marketed.
Principle	A rule or ethical standard.
Private Labeling	A retailer's name, as used on a product sold by the retailer but manufactured by another company.
Private Placement	The sale of shares directly to an institutional investor, such as a bank, mutual fund, insurance company, pension fund, or foundation.

Private Placement Disclaimer	A disclaimer that specifies that the sale of securities directly to an institutional investor, such as a bank, mutual fund, foundation, insurance company, etc. does not require Securities Exchange Commission (SEC) registration, provided that the securities are purchased for investment purchases only, not for resale.
Pro Forma	Description of financial statements that have one or more assumptions or hypothetical conditions built into the data. Often used with balance sheets and income statements when data is not available, to construct scenarios. One variety is called a Pro Forma Income Statement. Another is a Pro Forma Invoice.
Profit	The positive gain from an investment or business operation after deducting all expenses.
Project Timeline	The internally allocated time frame of a project from start to finish.
Promissory Note	A document signed by a borrower promising to repay a loan under agreed-upon terms. Also called a note.
Proof of Concept	Evidence from a market test or trial period that demonstrates that a business model or idea is feasible.
Publicity	Information that attracts attention to a business, product, person, or event.
R&D	Acronym for Research and Development.
Ratio Analysis	The study and interpretation of the relationships between various financial variables, used often by investors or lenders.
Research	The process of acquiring and organizing information for the purpose of initiating, modifying or terminating a particular investment or group of investments.
Research and Development	Acquiring new knowledge about products, processes, and services, and then applying that knowledge to create new and improved products, processes, and services that fill the needs of the market.

Résumé

A brief written synopsis of an individual's education, work experience, and accomplishments, typically for the purposes of finding a job. Also called a curriculum vitae, or CV.

Revenue

The total amount of money received by an organization for goods or services provided during a certain time period. Sometimes called turnover.

Risk

The quantifiable probability of loss or less-than-expected returns.

Robot.txt

Commonly called a Robots Exclusion Protocol, this is a convention to prevent cooperating web crawlers and other web robots from accessing all or part of a website which is otherwise publicly viewable. Also called Robot Exclusion Standard.

RSS Feed

Acronym for RDF Site Summary (although most commonly dubbed "Really Simple Syndication"). A congregation of web feed formats used to publish and automatically syndicate frequently updated works, such as blog entries, news headlines, audio, and video, in a standardized format.

S-Corporation

A type of corporation, recognized in the US by the Internal Revenue Service for most companies with 75 or fewer shareholders, which enables the company to enjoy the benefits of incorporation but be taxed as if it were a partnership. Also called Subchapter S Corporation, or S-Corp.

Sales

Total monetary amount collected for goods and services provided.

Sales Activity

The act of selling.

Sales Force

A group of people whose only corporate responsibility is to sell a company's products or services.

Sales Force Strategy

The strategic plan of a sales force to penetrate and have lasting impact on the market.

SBA

Acronym for the Small Business Administration in the US.

SBA Loan	A business loan issued by the US Small Business Administration.
Search Engine	Designed to search for information on the World Wide Web, search engines generally produce results presented in a list, often referred to as search engine results pages (SERPs). The information may consist of web pages, images, information and other types of files.
Search Engine Optimization	The process of improving the popularity of a website or a web page in search engines' un-paid ("natural") search results. In general, the earlier (or higher ranked on the search results page), and more frequently a site appears in the search results list, the more visitors it will receive from the search engine's users.
SEO	Acronym for search engine optimization.
Server	A physical computer hardware system dedicated to running one or more services, as a host, to serve the needs of users of the other computers on the network.
Shareholder	One who owns shares of stock in a corporation or mutual fund. For corporations, along with the ownership comes a right to declared dividends and the right to vote on certain company matters, including the board of directors. Also called a stockholder.
Site Traffic	The amount and flow of visitors to a website.
Small Business Administration	A US Federal agency which offers loans to small businesses.
Social Media	Web-based and mobile technologies used to turn communication into interactive dialogue between organizations, communities, and individuals. They are ubiquitously accessible, and enabled by scalable communication techniques.
Socioeconomics	Referring to social and economic conditions, social classes and income groups.

Software   A accumulation of computer programs and related data that provides the instructions that tell a computer what to do and how to do it.

Sole Proprietorship A company which is not registered with the state as a limited liability company or corporation and is a business structure in which an individual and his/her company are considered a single entity for tax and liability purposes.

Stakeholder   Anyone who is interested in or affected by something; one who could benefit from information about it. Not to be confused with shareholders.

Start-up   1. The beginning of a new company or new product. 2. A new, usually small business that is just beginning its operations, especially a new business supported by venture capital and in a sector where new technologies are used.

Start-up Capital   The initial stage in financing a new project, which is followed by several rounds of investment capital as the project gets under way

Statement of Cash Flows A summary of a company's cash flow over a given period of time. Also called Cash Flow Statement.

Stock Symbol   Ticker symbol for a stock.

Strategy   A planned system of action.

Strengths   Actions a business accomplishes exceptionally or easily; assets.

Subsidy   Financial aid given by the government to individuals or groups.

Surety Bond   A bond issued by an entity on behalf of a second party, guaranteeing that the second party will fulfill an obligation or series of obligations to a third party. In the event that the obligations are not met, the third party can recover its losses via the bond.

SWOT Analysis   An assessment of an organization's strengths, weaknesses, opportunities and threats.

Synopsis   A summary.

Takeover	Acquiring control of a corporation, called a target, by stock purchase or exchange, either hostile or friendly.
Target Market	The selection of a market that will be the most advantageous segment in which to offer a product or service. Also called a market target.
Tax Implications	Conditions or actions that can affect the amount of taxes payable.
Taxes	A fee levied (charged) by a government on a product, income, or activity.
Ticker	A scrolling display of current or recent security prices and/or volume.
Time Management	The act or process of planning and exercising conscious control over the amount of time spent on specific activities, especially to increase effectiveness, efficiency or productivity.
Trademark	A distinctive name, symbol, motto, or design that legally identifies a company or its products and services, and sometimes prevents others from using identical or similar marks.
Trade Secret	A formula, process, system, tool, etc. which provides a company with a competitive advantage.
Trading Platform	Software provided by a stock broker in order to buy and sell shares in the stock market.
Trend Analysis	A comparative analysis of a company's financial ratios over time.
Trends	The current general direction of movement for prices or rates. Also, increasingly frequent or widespread behavior.
Underwriting	The procedure by which an underwriter brings a new security issue to the investing public in an offering. In such a case, the underwriter will guarantee a certain price for a certain number of securities to the party that is issuing the security. Thus, the issuer is secure that they will raise a certain minimum from the issue, while the underwriter bears the risk of the issue.

Uniform Resource Locator	A specific character string that constitutes a reference to an Internet resource, usually by its acronym, URL.
United States Copyright Office	The US Government body that maintains records of copyright registration in the United States.
United States Patent and Trademark Office	An agency in the United States Department of Commerce that issues patents to inventors and businesses for their inventions, and trademark registration for product and intellectual property identification.
URL	Acronym for Uniform Resource Locator.
USCO	Acronym for United States Copyright Office.
USPTO	Acronym for United States Patent and Trademark Office.
Variable Expense	A cost of labor, material or overhead that changes according to the change in the volume of production units. Combined with fixed costs, variable costs make up the total cost of production. Also called variable cost.
Venture Capitalist	An investor who engages in venture capital projects. Venture capitalists seek opportunities involving businesses that are growing or are in risky market segments, since these businesses generally have a harder time obtaining loans. Frequently called VCs.
Virtual Receptionist	An outsourced call-handling person trained to manage your calls exactly as an in-house employee would, but from another location.
Voice-Over Internet Protocol	Commonly refers to the communication protocols, technologies, methodologies, and transmission techniques involved in the delivery of voice communications and multimedia sessions over Internet Protocol (IP) networks, such as the World Wide Web.
VOIP	Acronym for Voice-Over Internet Protocol.

Web Analytics	The measurement, accumulation, analysis and reporting of Internet data for purposes of understanding and optimizing web usage.
Web-Based	Of, relating to, or using the World Wide Web.
Web-Based Business	A company that does most of its business on the Internet, usually through a website that uses the popular top-level domain, *.com*. Also called an Internet business, web business, dot-com company, or simply a dot-com.
Web Hosting	A type of Internet service that allows individuals and organizations to make their website accessible via the World Wide Web.
Webmaster	A person responsible for maintaining one or many websites. Also called a web architect, web developer, site author, or website administrator.
Wholesale	The purchase of goods in quantity for resale purposes. Also called wholesale distribution.
Wholesale Distribution	See *wholesale*.
Working Capital	Current liabilities subtracted from current assets. Working capital measures the liquid assets a company has available to build its business.

Resources

ExpertBusinessAdvice.com

At **ExpertBusinessAdvice.com**, our goal is to become your complete resource for simple, easy-to-use business information and resources. Enjoy reading about techniques and processes necessary to develop and grow your business. **ExpertBusinessAdvice.com** offers an array of tools and resources to help you along the way by offering tutorials, downloadable templates, real-life examples, and customer support. You can even email us and a qualified member of our staff (yes, a real person!) will review your inquiry and get back to you within 24 hours. Now you can take charge of your professional growth and development, learn from others' success, and make a dramatic positive impact on your business. Learn the principles and practices that seasoned professionals use, at **ExpertBusinessAdvice.com,** for free!

THE WAY FORWARD BEGINS HERE...

Want to learn how to start a business? Are you looking for an additional income stream? No problem—we can get you started down the right path. Do you want to know how to plan, creating the necessary documents to obtain financing for your business? Maybe you just want to learn how experienced business leaders streamline financial models, maximize output, inspire managers, and incentivize employees, tapping the full range of resources available. Regardless of your needs, **ExpertBusinessAdvice.com** is here for you!

www.expertbusinessadvice.com

CRASH COURSE for ENTREPRENEURS

Many novice entrepreneurs have little more than a brilliant idea and a pocketful of ambition. They want to know *Now what?* This 12-title series tells *exactly what you must know*, in simple terms, using real-world examples. Each two-hour read walks you through a key aspect of being an entrepreneur and gives practical, seasoned, reader-friendly advice.

Whether your dream business is dog walking or high-tech invention, home-based or web-based, these books will save you time and trouble as you set up and run your new company. Collectively, these three young Florida-based serial entrepreneurs have successfully started seventeen new companies across a broad range of sectors and frameworks, including finance, international sourcing, medical products, innovative dot-com initiatives, and traditional brick-and-mortar companies.

A Crash Course for Entrepreneurs—From Expert Business Advice

Starting a Business – Everything you need to build a new business, starting from scratch.
Sales and Marketing – Solid guidance on successfully developing and promoting your business and its brand.
Managing Your Business – Proven techniques in managing employees and guiding your business in the right direction.
Business Finance – Tax tips, funding resources, money management, basic accounting, and more!
Legal Aspects of Entrepreneurship – A must-know overview on types of businesses, risks and liabilities, required documents, regulatory requirements, and the role of a business attorney. *Co-Author: Mark R. Moon, Esq.*
Franchising – A how-to guide for buying and running a franchise business.
Value-Driven Business – Value is the muscle behind every successful business. Here's how to introduce it into your operation.
Time and Efficiency – Wheel-spinning is the most destructive force in business. Make the most of your time to maximize income and motivate employees.
International Business – The world is a big place filled with billions of potential partners and customers. This guide offers tips to reach them all.
Supplemental Income – Can't commit full time? No problem! Here's how to make extra money in your spare time.
Social Media – This rapidly-growing networking and advertising medium is changing the world. Here's how to use it to grow your business.
Web-Based Business – The biggest, most valuable companies out there today are Internet businesses. Here's why, and how you can build one yourself.
Paperback and eBook format available. 160 pages, 6 ½" × 9" (16.5 × 23 cm), US$18.95, with extensive glossary and index.

www.expertbusinessadvice.com   www.novavistapub.com

Index

Tip: We suggest that you check the Glossary (pages 123-145) for definitions related to items you want to look up in this index.

301 re-direct 88

A

Accounting 13, 28, 70, 74, 87, 103-04, 107
Accounting representation 103-4, 107
Accredited investor 64
Acquisitions 50
Advertising 36, 47, 101-02
Analysis 35, 41, 43, 51, 81, 86, 103
Analytics (websites) 115-16
Angel investors 34, 64, 68-71
Angel groups or networks 70
Attorney 59
Audience See *Target market or audience.*

B

Balance sheets 103
Banks 67-71
Bid bond 95
Blogs 140
Blue chip 83-84
Board of directors 45-46
Bonds
  Bid 95
  Indemnity 95
  License 95
  Payment 95
  Performance 95
  Security 95
  Surety 95-96

Bookkeeping 59, 87, 97, 103, 107
Bottom line 101
Bounce rates 116
Brand, branding 43, 85-87, 90, 105-06, 136
Brick-and-mortar 113
Browser emulators 116
Business angel 70
Business development incentives 65
Business licenses 29-30
Business model 41, 80, 114, 132, 139
Business plan 24, 32, 35-52, 55, 59-60, 67, 69, 113
  How to write 35-52
Business plan elements
  Appendix 37, 42, 51-52
  Company description 36, 44
  Executive summary 35, 39-41
  Financials 37, 50-51
  Funding request 35-36, 39, 49
  Market analysis 35, 41-44
  Marketing and sales strategies 36, 47-48
  Organization and management 36, 45-47
  Service or product line 36, 41, 43-44, 48-49
Buying patterns, buyers 42, 102, 114

C

Capital 33, 63-64, 67, 80
Capital expenditures 50, 74
Cash 75
Cash capital disbursements 64
Cash flow statements 98, 103

C-Corporation 27-28
Chat rooms 114
Class A office space 84
Collateral 50, 63, 71, 114
Common challenges for entrepreneurs 97-98
Communication strategy 47
Company description 35, 44
Competition 19-20, 36, 41, 43-44, 48-9, 55, 65, 85, 98, 101-02, 113-14, 119
Contact emails 84
Contact list 116
Contracts 26, 30, 52, 64, 70-71, 87, 95, 104
Controlling interest 64
Copyright 25-26, 32, 49, 60, 8-90
Corporate logo See *Logos.*
Corporate management 36, 45-47
Corporation See *C-Corporation, S-Corporation, Limited Liability Company (LLC), Professional Limited Liability Company (PLLC).*
Crawl simulation programs 105, 116
Creativity 59
Credentials 109
Credit 51, 67-68, 70-71, 73-75
Credit reports
    History 67-68
    Business 74
    Personal 73
    Transferability 74
Credit score 73
Curriculum vitae (résumé) 37, 45, 51, 129
Customers 23, 36, 41, 43, 46-48, 58, 92-93, 96, 98, 114, 119, 146
Customer service or support 84, 102, 104, 114, 146

D
Database 114
Debt 63, 70
Debt financing 63
Debt retirement (repaying loans) 50, 63, 71
Debt-to-income ratio 73-74
Decision making 20

Demographics 41-42
Distribution channels 47
Distribution strategy 47, 113
Dividends 28
Domain name 87

E
E-commerce 113-14
Economy 19, 55
Entrepreneurial traits 19-20
Equipment 47, 50, 57, 63=64, 84
Equity 47, 49, 63-64 67-68, 70
Equity financing 63-64, 67
European Patent Office (EPO) 91
Executive summary 35, 39-41
Execution 79 See also *Planning.*
Expansion capital 60
Expenses 23, 37, 50, 64, 113
Expert Business Advice 119, 121, 146-47

F
Fair Isaac Corporation (FICO) 73
Family and friends, financing from 69-71
Financial data 69-71
    Historical 50
    Prospective (future-oriented) 50-51
Financial strategies 49
Financing 24, 39, 63-75, 113
    How to obtain 63-65
Focus 40, 48, 53-54, 56, 68, 70, 80, 102, 104, 158
Follow-through 53
Franchising 37, 147
Funding request 35-36, 39, 49

G
General partnership 27-28, 33
Getting business and customers 101-02
Going public See *Initial public offering.*
Grants 64
Graphic design See *Logos.*
Great idea 23, 25-27, 36, 39, 44, 49, 53-54, 57-58, 60, 89, 91-92, 113, 147
Gross margin 42

Government funding 64
Growth rate 41
Growth strategy 47

H
Hiring 109-10
Home-based business 13, 29-30
Hyperlinks See *Links.*

I
Idea for a business See *Great idea.*
Income statements 37, 51
Incorporating 28 See also *Corporation* for types.
Incubator office space 84
Indemnity bond 95
Informal investor 70
Initial public offering (IPO) 55-56, 64, 71
Insurance 95
Intellectual property (IP) 25, 44, 89-90, 92
Interest in business (ownership) 64-65
Interest on loan 64, 67, 70-71, 74
Internet business See *Web-based business.*
Internet marketing See *Web-based marketing.*
Interview 109
Investment groups 64
Investor 33-34, 64, 67 69, 87

J-K
Keywords, keyword phrases 87-88, 106

L
Leader 20-21, 40, 81, 104 157
Leads (sales) 48
Lead time 43
Legal representation 103-04
Lending 67-68
Leveraged buyout 50
Liability 27-28, 34, 63
License bond 95
Licensing See *Business licenses.*
Limited liability company (LLC) 27-28, 34, 36

Links (hyperlinks) 106, 116
Liquidity 75
Listening 20
Loans 63-64, 67-68, 71, 73
    Cash capital disbursement 64
    Interest on 64, 67, 70-71, 74
    Scoring system for 73
    Terms for repaying 50, 63-64, 70-71, 73-74
Location 23
Logos, logo designers 25, 32, 85-86, 98, 105
Losses 103
Loyalty 109-10

M
Mailbox shops (Mailboxes Etc., UPS) 83
Management team 45
Market analysis 35, 41
Marketing 24, 31-32, 36-37, 42, 47, 53, 89-90, 97, 101-02, 105, 114-15
    E-marketing 113-14 See also *Web-based marketing.*
    Traditional 101
Marketing plan 24, 32, 37
Marketing strategy 36, 47, 117
Market penetration 36, 47
Market share 42-43, 101-02
Market testing 22, 24, 41, 57-58, 60
Media 15, 36, 42, 101-02, 106, 115
Merchant banking 113
Mission statement 36, 40
Motivation 19
Multimedia 106

N
Naming a company, product or service 31-32
Network 42, 59-60, 70, 102
Non-disclosure agreement (NDA) 26

O
Office space 83-84
Online marketing See *Web-based marketing.*
Outsourcing 37, 107
Over-saturated market See *Competition.*
Owner-operated 27

P

Partners 27-28, 33-34, 47, 64
Partnership 27-28, 33-34, 46, 103
Passion 14-15
Patent 25, 49, 60, 89-93
    Australian 91
Payment bond 95
Percentage of ownership 34, 64
Performance bond 95
Permits See *Licensing a business.*
Personal finances 23-24
Planning, preparation 19-66, 79-81, 103, 113
Positive cash flow 63
Press release 106-07, 117
Pricing 42-43, 114
Principal of a loan 64
Prioritizing 55-56
Private labeling 37
Private placement disclaimer 57, 67
Product description See *Service or product line description.*
Professional Limited Liability Company (PLLC) 28
Profits 28, 33, 50, 56-58, 64, 102, 107
Pro forma 37
Projections 51, 67-68
Project timeline 80-81
Promissory note 63
Prospective (future-oriented) data 68 See also *Projections.*
Publicity 31 See also *Press release, Marketing.*

Q

Query (on the web) 87-88, 114

R

Receptionist, virtual 84
Repayment of loans See *Loans.*
Research 22, 24, 36-37, 41-43, 57-58, 60, 63-65, 70, 75, 79, 102, 113-14
Research and development (R&D) 49
Résumé (curriculum vita) 37, 45, 51, 129
Retrospective data 68

Return on investment (ROI) 67, 69-70
Revenue 27, 36-37, 46, 64, 80, 98, 113
Risk and reward 63-64, 69-71
RSS feeds (RDF Site Summary, also "Really Simple Syndication") 116

S

S-Corporation 27-28
Sales 50, 63, 67, 84, 88, 101, 114
    And market share 28, 102
    Sales activity 48
    Sales strategy 36-37, 46-48
Search engine 36, 87, 105-06, 115
Search engine optimization (SEO) 36, 105-06, 115-17
Seed money (start-up capital) 23, 64, 80
Service or product line description 48
Sectors of industry 28, 35, 65, 70
Security 24, 26, 70, 92, 114 See also *Collateral.*
Security bond 95
Site traffic
Small Business Administration (SBA, in the US) loans 65
Slogans 90, 105, 119
Social media 15, 101-02, 106, 115
Sole proprietorship 27, 36, 46, 103
Speed of business 79 See also *Stage of business.*
Spiders (on websites) 36
Stage of business 79-81
    Decline 79-80
    Development 79-80
    Maintenance 79-80
    Start-up 79-80
    Turnaround 79, 81
    See also *Speed of business.*
Start-up capital 23, 64, 80
Strategy, strategic advantage 24, 26, 28, 36, 47-48, 50, 59-60, 92, 101, 105-06, 109
Subsidies 64-65
Surety bond 95-96
Surfing the Internet 87, 114
SWOT, or competitive analysis (strengths, weaknesses, opportunities, threats) 43

T

Takeover 47, 50, 64

Talent 109-10

Target market or audience 35, 40-44, 48, 87, 102, 105

Taxes 27-28, 34, 57-58, 74, 107-08
    Documentation for 108

Timelines 80

Time management 97 See also *Prioritizing.*

Trade secrets 49

Trademark 25-26, 32, 44, 60, 85, 89-93

Trading platform 65

Transition from employee to entrepreneur 24

Trends 36, 41-42, 51, 101, 119

Type of business 20-22, 27, 36, 46

U

Uniform Resource Locator (URL) 87-88, 102

US Copyright Office (USCO) 90

US Patent and Trademark Office (USPTO) 90-93

URL 87-88, 102

Utility patent 92

V

Venture capitalists (VCs) 64-65, 67-71

Viewers or visitors 105, 116

Voice-over internet protocol (VOIP) 84

Virtual receptionists, voice-over (VO) phone greetings 84

W

Web analytics 115-16

Web-based marketing or business 101-02, 113-17

Webmaster program 116

Website hosting 113

Website 13, 25, 29, 36, 70, 84, 87-88, 90-93, 102, 106, 113-117, 119

Website viewers or visitors 105, 116

Will-power, self-discipline 20

Wholesale distribution 36-37, 47, 89, 113

Working capital 50

Y-Z

Zoning requirements 30

About the Authors

Scott L. Girard, Jr.

Editor-in-Chief, Expert Business Advice, LLC
Email: scott@expertbusinessadvice.com

Before joining Expert Business Advice, Scott was Executive Vice President of Pinpoint Holdings Group, Inc., where he directed multiple marketing and advertising initiatives. Scott was a key player for the Group, negotiating and facilitating the sourcing logistics for the commercial lighting industry division, which supplied clients such as Gaylord Palms, Ritz Carlton, Marriott, Mohegan Sun, and Isle of Capri with large-scale lighting solutions. His vision and work were also pivotal in the growth and development of Bracemasters International, LLC.

Scott has degrees in Business Administration and English Writing and is a published contributor to various periodicals on the topics of economics and politics. He is also a co-author and series editor of *A Crash Course for Entrepreneurs* book series. A graduate of the United States Army Officer Candidate School, Scott is a combat veteran, having served a tour in Kuwait and Iraq as an infantry platoon leader in support of Operation Iraqi Freedom and Operation New Dawn.

Originally from Glendale, California, Scott now lives in St. Petersburg, Florida with his wife. Scott is a regular contributor to www.expertbusiness.com. His side projects include a collection of fiction short stories and scripts for two feature films. His motto: "Words have meaning."

Michael F. O'Keefe

Officer, Expert Business Advice, LLC
Email: mike@expertbusinessadvice.com

In 2004, Mike founded O'Keefe Motor Sports, Inc. (OMS Superstore), eventually growing it into the largest database of aftermarket automotive components available for online purchase in the world. Currently, aside from his position at Expert

Business Advice, LLC, Mike is President of Pinpoint Holdings Group, Inc. and Vice President of Marketing for Bracemasters International, LLC.

At Pinpoint, Mike's focus is building a strong base for understanding the global marketplace. He also plays a key role in facilitating the logistics of the commercial lighting branch of the company, bridging between Pinpoint's office in Wuxi, China, and their commercial clients—hotel chains such as Gaylord Palms, Ritz Carlton, Marriott, Mohegan Sun and Isle of Capri.

Recently, Mike's passion and talents for cutting-edge business techniques and practices have led to the exponential growth of Bracemasters. By developing web-based marketing strategies and E-commerce initiatives, as well as formatting on-line documents that enabled the company to reach a vast number of current and potential patient-customers, Mike increased Bracemasters' website viewership by 17,000% in two years.

Originally from Delavan, Wisconsin, Mike now lives in Orlando, Florida. He is a regular contributor to www.expertbusiness.com. His motto: "Rome did not create a great empire by having meetings; they did it by killing all those who opposed them."

Marc A. Price

Director of Operations, Expert Business Advice, LLC
Email: marc@expertbusinessadvice.com

Marc has collaborated with the Federal Government, United States Military, major non-profit organizations, and some of the largest corporations in America, developing and implementing new products, services and educational programs. Equally skilled in Business-to-Business and Business-to-Consumer functions, Marc has facilitated product positioning, branding and outreach efforts on many different platforms for the organizations he has worked with.

As an entrepreneur, Marc has successfully directed the launch of seven different companies, ranging from traditional brick-and-mortar establishments to innovative dot-com initiatives. Four were entertainment production companies (sound, lighting, staging, logistics, talent, entertainment), one was a business services company serving small companies, one was concerned with business and land acquisition, and two were website and business consulting services. Using his expertise in organizational management and small business development, Marc's latest focus is on working with new entrepreneurs and small-to-medium-sized businesses in emerging industries.

As an accomplished public speaker and writer, Marc has appeared on nationally syndicated television and radio networks, in national print publications, and has been the subject of numerous interviews and special-interest stories. Marc is a regular contributor to ExpertBusinessAdvice.com.

Marc received his Bachelor of Science in Organizational Management from Ashford University. He and his wife divide time between Orlando, Florida and elsewhere, including an active schedule of international travel. His motto: "You can't build a reputation on what you are going to do."—Henry Ford

Business Efficiency Resources

Get More Done Seminars

Grooms Consulting Group, a sister company to Nova Vista Publishing, offers proven training that saves professionals one month or more of time wasted on email, information and meeting inefficiency.

- 83% of all professionals are overloaded by email – we can save up to 3 weeks a year, per person
- 92% want to improve their information storage system – we can make searches 25% faster and more successful
- 43% of all meeting time is wasted – we can save up to another 3 weeks per year, per person

"We saved 15 days a year!"
Matt Koch, Director of Productivity
Capital One Financial Services

Three Two-Hour Modules: We offer three powerful seminars: **Get Control of Email, Get Control of Info,** and **Get Control of Meetings.**
They can be delivered in any combination you wish and can be customized.
Who Should Attend? Anyone who handles email, stores information, and attends meetings. Leaders leverage their position for added impact.
Delivery Options: Seminar, keynote speech, webinar, e-learning, and executive coaching.
Return on Investment (ROI): We can measure the impact of every session on participants with five-minute online pre- and post-surveys. We deliver a report that shows time saved, productivity gained, participant satisfaction, and other significant impacts.

Special pricing is available for groups.

Three Get More Done Modules: Combine and Customize as You Wish

1. GET CONTROL OF EMAIL
- Pump up your productivity by eliminating unnecessary email
- De-clutter your jammed inbox
- Write more effective messages
- Discover time-saving Outlook® / Lotus® tech tips
- Improve email etiquette and reduce legal liability
- Choose the best communication tool

2. GET CONTROL OF INFORMATION
- Get organized, once and for all
- Never lose a document again
- File and find your information in a flash; make shared drives productive
- Make better decisions with the right information
- Create an ordered, stress-free folder structure throughout your system

3. GET CONTROL OF MEETINGS
- Meet less and do more through virtual and other advanced options
- Reduce costs, boost productivity and go green with improved, efficient virtual meetings
- Run engaging, productive live meetings
- Discover time-saving e-calendar tips
- Keep every meeting productive and on track, make follow-ups easy

Satisfaction Guaranteed
We guarantee that the vast majority of your people will rate our seminars "excellent" or "good," or your money back.

"A huge hit with our people!"
Joel Burkholder
Regional Program Coordinator – ACLCP

Contact: Kathe Grooms
kgrooms@groomsgroup.com

TWO MUST-READ BOOKS FOR ENTREPRENEURS

Win-Win Selling: Turning Customer NEEDS into SALES

Differentiating your company's products and services is a big challenge today. But a company's sales force can become a significant differentiator, and gain sustainable advantages, if it adopts the Counselor approach. A win-win mind and skill set, based on trust, problem-solving and side-by-side work between seller and customer, makes buying easy. And because the seller stays by the customer after the sale, the door opens for long-term, expanding business.

Fortune 500 global and other companies in 30 countries have used Wilson Learning's Counselor approach for years with astonishing success. The book gives the million-plus people who have taken Wilson Learning's *The Counselor Salesperson* workshop a refresher, and gives others a powerful sales process. The Foreword is by Larry Wilson, author of *One Minute Salesperson* and founder of Wilson Learning (1965). It's an indispensable book for salespeople and sales managers, who agree it's solid, practical and really works.

"The Counselor Approach enhanced our leadership position by helping our sales and marketing organization discover what is most important in our marketplace. As a result, we are adding value to our customers as a means of advocating for the patient."

Dan Schlewitz, Vice President Sales, Medtronic CRM

Win-Win Selling (ISBN for Third Edition 978-90-77256-34-3).
160 pages, softcover, 160 × 230 cm (6" × 9").
Suggested retail price: € 18.95, US$18.95
Models, charts, anecdotes, an index and other resources.

Social Styles Handbook: Adapt Your Style to Win Trust

Backed by a database of more than 2 million people, Wilson Learning's Social Styles concepts are powerful, life-changing communication tools. The ways people prefer to influence others and how they feel about showing emotion identify them as Analyticals, Expressives, Drivers or Amiables. You feel comfortable acting within your own style. But to relate to others well, you must consciously adjust your style to theirs. That's Versatility, which improves performance in every aspect of your work and life.

Find your style and learn to recognize others'. Understand and appreciate the strengths and differences in each. Learn how to become Versatile while still being yourself. Important tools for recognizing tension and Back-Up Behavior and handling it productively, plus techniques for influencing others, have made this a best-selling book that delivers results.

"I'm not sure I can quantify the value of using Social Styles, but I know I would not want to do my job without it."

Ann Horner, Main Board Director, Bourne Leisure Limited

Social Styles Handbook (ISBN Revised Edition 978-90-77256-33-6)
192 pages, softcover, 160 × 230 cm (6" × 9").
Suggested retail price: € 19.95, US$19.95
Models, charts, anecdotes, an index and other resources.

Now available in eBook formats!
www.novavistapub.com

CAREERS
I Just Love My Job!
Roy Calvert, Brian Durkin, Eugenio Grandi and Kevin Martin, in the Quarto Consulting Library (ISBN 978-90-77256-02-2, softcover, 192 pages, $19.95)

Taking Charge of Your Career
Leigh Bailey (ISBN 978-90-77256-13-8, softcover, 96 pages, $14.95)

LEADERSHIP AND INNOVATION
Grown-Up Leadership
Leigh Bailey and Maureen Bailey (ISBN 978-90-77256-09-1, softcover, 144 pages, $18.95)

Grown-Up Leadership Workbook
Leigh Bailey (ISBN 978-90-77256-15-2, softcover, 96 pages, $14.95)

Leading Innovation
Brian McDermott and Gerry Sexton (ISBN 978-90-77256-05-3, softcover, 160 pages, $18.95)

Time Out for Leaders
Donald Luce and Brian McDermott (ISBN 978-90-77256-30-5 softcover, $14.95)

SALES
Time Out for Salespeople
Nova Vista Publishing's Best Practices Editors, (ISBN 978-90-77256-14-5 hardcover with marker ribbon, 272 pages, $19.95; ISBN 978-90-77256-31-2 softcover, 272 pages, $14.95)

Get-Real Selling, Revised Edition
Michael Boland and Keith Hawk (ISBN 978-90-77256-32-9, softcover, 144 pages, $18.95)

CUSTOMER SERVICE AND ORGANIZATIONAL TRANSFORMATION
Service Excellence @ Novell
Nova Vista Publishing's Best Practices Editors (ISBN 978-90-77256-11-4 softcover, 112 pages, $18.95)

SCIENCE PARKS, ECONOMICS, ECOLOGY OF INNOVATION
What Makes Silicon Valley Tick?
Tapan Munroe, Ph.D., with Mark Westwind, MPA (ISBN 978-90-77256-28-2, softcover, 192 pages, $19.95)

Visit www.novavistapub.com for sample chapters, reviews, links and ordering.
E-books are now available too!